MANCHESTER LINERS

- an extraordinary story

by

Nick Robins

FOREWORD: MANCHESTER LINERS FROM THE BRIDGE OF A HARRISON LINE SHIP

While Harrison officers and crews were well used to the port of Manchester and its Canal, we certainly saw Manchester Liners as 'the home team'. In the early days we saw the strong looking, stoutly built Manchester Liners of the **Manchester Port**-class berthed at the top end of Number 9 Dock. Clearly built for the North Atlantic, and considering they were in a bad weather trade, always smart and well maintained. We always felt that Manchester Liners received preferential treatment in the Canal and the docks at Manchester and it used to be said that if there was one of their ships moving anywhere in the canal, everything else stopped. All over the city of Manchester its ships were known simply as 'The Liners'. But we used to giggle on walking past the 'liners' late at night to see only the light of a hurricane lamp on the gangway due to the boilers being shutdown with no other illumination anywhere on the whole ship. One way of saving money and letting the men all go home at night!

ML's greatest initiative was its move to containers when it commissioned and operated the first British ocean-going container ships of the famous **Manchester Challenge**-class of 1968. All very new with no established patterns and designs to follow and at a time when many British shipping companies had not yet even decided whether containerised transport was viable. Red hulls with the bridge, engines and deckhouse fully aft, a new type of engine, and with a cargo consisting of only containers worked from specially constructed terminals on both sides of the Atlantic.

We in Harrisons, and probably others, looked upon these red ships and their red containers with some scepticism. Somehow they were not quite seaman-like and almost a bit 'sissy'. Little did we know that this was the start of a revolution which in less than 30 years would sweep almost all the British seafarers from the oceans and with it the grand shipping companies we knew so well, including Manchester Liners.

Captain Michael D R Jones, Ainsdale, Lancs.

Published by Bernard McCall, 400 Nore Road, Portishead, Bristol, BS20 8EZ, England.
Telephone/fax : 01275 846178   E-mail : bernard@coastalshipping.co.uk   Website : www.coastalshipping.co.uk
All distribution enquiries should be addressed to the publisher.

Printed by Short Run Press Ltd, 25 Bittern Road, Sowton Industrial Estate, Exeter, EX2 7LW
Telephone : 01392 211909; fax : 01392 444134
E-mail : info@shortrunpress.co.uk   Website : www.shortrunpress.co.uk

ISBN : 978-1-902953-55-7

FRONT COVER : Courage was displayed by directors and staff of Manchester Liners in peace and in war throughout the company's existence. It is appropriate that the 1969-built **Manchester Courage** features on both front and back covers. On the front we see the ship in a classic setting as she approaches the entrance to the Manchester Ship Canal at Eastham on a sunny 12 August 1976.

[Laurie Schofield]

BACK COVER : By contrast we see the same vessel in the shadow of the Quebec Bridge as the thaw sets in and melts the wintry ice.

[Manchester Liners Limited]

FRONTISPIECE : The view from the bridge looking forward, the **Manchester Miller** [1959] in ice.

[Derrick Howarth]

PREFACE

Manchester Liners was created with help from Sir Christopher Furness in 1898 to demonstrate the viability of the new Manchester Ship Canal for liner traffic. From the outset its core product was a seasonal service between Manchester and Montreal and, when the St Lawrence was frozen over, St John, New Brunswick. Connecting services were arranged into the Great Lakes ports, and diversification with routes to the eastern seaboard and southern US states helped develop a strong company. Eventually Manchester Liners sailed its own 'Lakers' from Manchester to Chicago, Detroit and Milwaukee, and once the St Lawrence Seaway opened in 1959 it sent its big ships directly into the Lakes to load grain for Manchester – inland Britain to inland Canada and the US. Having achieved all this Manchester Liners decided to containerise, being one of only two European shipping companies to make this bold move without first joining a consortium to spread the costs and associated risks.

The people involved in driving the company are fascinating. The first Managing Director was Robert Stoker and he succeeded Sir Christopher Furness as the second Chairman. Stoker was in time succeeded on the Board, and as both MD and Chairman, by his son Kenneth and grandson Rob. There was a Stoker in the Directorship until Rob Stoker stepped down from the role of Chairman in 1979. Shortly afterwards the company became a Furness Withy subsidiary and was slowly submerged within the Furness Withy Shipping Division after the 'great Chinese take-away' when CY Tung acquired Furness and its subsidiaries in 1980.

The triumphs and the failures of the company are recounted with an emphasis on the human story. The link with the City of Manchester underlines the important role both Manchester Liners and the Manchester Ship Canal Company had in wealth creation in the north-west of England during the twentieth century.

I am particularly grateful to author Marianne Pilgrim for permission to reproduce abstracts from her novel *The Memoires of Virginia Lord*, and to Lilian Frier for permission to include an abstract from a description of the *Manchester Shore Gang* by her late husband, Peter, first published in the Manchester Liners Old Shipmates Association (MLOSA) web pages at http://manchesterliners.co.uk . Indeed the help given by webmaster Derrick Howarth in seeking permission to use various images published on the MLOSA site is also most gratefully acknowledged and individual copyright holders are cited in the respective captions wherever these are known. I must thank Ian Ramsay, Captain Michael Jones, Captain Peter Cullen and Chris Robins for critically reviewing the manuscript, each from different angles, and various correspondents who have helped answer my enquiries to assist in exposing this remarkable and innovative part of British maritime history. Finally my thanks must go to publisher Bernard McCall, to Gil Mayes and Iain McCall who have done sterling work in checking initial drafts of the book and to the staff of 4Word Ltd and Short Run Press for their work in the production of the finished book.

Dr Nick Robins
Crowmarsh, Oxfordshire

September 2011

CONTENTS

As will be explained on page 46, the names of the ships were chosen with care. Expressing a combination of optimism and vibrency, the **Manchester Vigour** leaves Eastham on 30 August 1979.

[Laurie Schofield]

The *Manchester City* (1898) was the biggest ship to travel the Manchester Ship Canal when she was first commissioned. She was also the world's biggest meat carrier at the time.

[John Clarkson]

Sheltering in the Cromarty Firth, shortly after commencing her maiden voyage, she was driven ashore eventually returning to the Tyne for repairs. The sorry tale is best described in the report of the Admiralty Court Hearing in January 1899:

*She left the Tyne on 29 October. On 31 October the quadrant over her rudder was carried away, and the vessel fell off before the wind, being at the time off Dunnet Head, Scotland. There was a hard gale. Both anchors were at once let go but the cables carried away and the vessel continued to drift to the eastward. The Orkney lifeboat came out. They [the crew] assisted the master [of the **Manchester City**] in pointing out the dangerous parts of the coast. As the **Manchester City** passed through the Pentland Firth the Thurso lifeboat came out and made fast. The **St Ola**, which was on a voyage from Wick to Stromness, with mails and passengers, also came out later with the **Jamesia** [fishing boat] but the attempts to make fast were unsuccessful owing to the rapidity with which the **Manchester City** drifted and they left her. The **Jamesia** subsequently returned and agreed to tow the Thurso lifeboat ashore for £6 which was paid and a receipt obtained.*

*About this time the tug **Tyne** also arrived. An agreement was entered into by which the master of the **Tyne** undertook to hold the **Manchester City** in her sheltered position off Duncansby Head until she could effect repairs and afterwards to tow her to a place of safety for £150, but in the event of the **Tyne** leaving the **Manchester City** before she was safely at anchor the agreement to be void...*

*...the **Manchester City** was proceeding towards the shore. After this a lifeboat which was lying alongside was found to hamper her movements and her crew were requested to cast off; and she returned to the Orkneys. On 1 November all hands commenced rigging temporary gear. Shortly afterwards the **Loch Lomond** [fishing vessel] came up and made fast astern to assist in the steering of the **Manchester City**. A course was then shaped for Cromarty Firth being assisted into the harbour by the **Earnholm** [coastal passenger steamer].*

*On 2 November the wind increasing, the wire hauser, by which she [the **Manchester City**] lay to her anchor, was carried away and she drifted ashore on Nigg Beach, where she remained pending the arrival of tugs ordered from the Tyne. On 4 November the **Hercules** and **Comet** arrived, but as a gale prevailed it was decided not to attempt towage off the bank until a more favourable opportunity occurred. Eventually she was got off the bank, and at 2 pm on 7 November, after several other accidents had taken place, she was moored at Jarrow Stake.*

The **Manchester City** first came up to Manchester in January 1899 while the Admiralty court hearing about her near loss in the Pentland Firth was in session. She carried 450 head of cattle and 150 sheep as well as grain and a mixed cargo manifest. R B Stoker in his brief history of the Company reported:

How there were many shakings of the head, not in Liverpool only, over the audacity of the attempt. How for the first half mile up the 'ditch' the idle spectators were rather worried but Pilot George Cartwright and Captain Forrest passed other vessels and brought her through the locks without scratching the paint. That night she stopped at Irlam to give the pilots, officers and engineers a well earned rest – the pilots 'looking as if they had not been in bed for a week, after they have finished the day's work, for their eyes are bleared with exhaustion'.

The following morning the **Manchester City** berthed alongside the Mode Wheel lairage and her officers and pilots were whisked away to the Town Hall for a full blown civic reception with the Lord Mayor. The essence of the celebration was that if a modern, large ocean cargo liner such as the **Manchester City** could safely navigate to Manchester, so could any of the vessels on the Pacific and Indian runs as well as those serving the Americas. As Stoker described it:

It was a great day for Manchester; the bogey that only medium-sized ships could navigate the canal was exorcised and the port was now able to attract the largest cargo ships then available.

The 8,000 ton deadweight **Manchester Merchant** and **Manchester Port** joined the fleet in May 1899 and February 1900 respectively, both products of Palmers' yard on the Tyne. The equally large 430 feet sisters **Manchester Corporation** and **Manchester Commerce** were delivered by the Furness, Withy shipyard at Middlesbrough in July and November 1899.

Looking aft aboard **Manchester Corporation** (1899) - note the small hatches and clear decks designed to shed water.

[Ray Carter courtesy of Neil Carter]

Cattle stalls on the Forward Main Deck of the **Manchester Corporation**.

[Ray Carter courtesy of Neil Carter]

The Houston Line (British & South American Steam Navigation Company) steamer **Hydaspes** (1899) was commissioned as the **Manchester Port** but only remained in ML colours for just over a year.

[Author's collection]

The **Manchester Shipper** (1900) was designed specifically for the Montreal service.

[John Clarkson]

And finally the smaller **Manchester Importer** and **Manchester Shipper** arrived from Irvine's yard at West Hartlepool in August 1899 and February 1900. It is notable that the owners had electric lighting fitted in all its ships at this time.

Experience with the new ships would show the 8,000 tonners to be difficult vessels to fill and the optimum tonnage for the Montreal service was nearer that of the smaller **Manchester Importer** and her sister. But Robert Stoker now had a fine fleet of modern vessels that were more than capable of maintaining the fortnightly departure from Manchester to Canada. The enlarged fleet provided some flexibility and calls by inducement were made at Liverpool and Queenstown, and in the summer months on the St Lawrence the ships could also put into Chicoutimi, Quebec, Rimouski and Charlottetown as required.

Before the turn of the century the company received the sad news of the loss of the **Manchester Enterprise**, the very first ship to fly the Manchester Liners' flag. During a storm she had developed a list to starboard and on the evening of 14 November it was realised that she was leaking. The Chief Engineer found that plates were being lifted by the rush of water in the athwartships bunker and he realised the difficulty the firemen were having in maintaining a satisfactory head of steam. The pumps were kept hard at work and for a time kept the water at bay until suddenly water began rushing through the starboard bunker door into the aft stokehold. By 7 pm the flow had increased and extinguished the fire for the starboard boiler. At 9.30 pm the firemen gave up and went to ask the Master what he was going to do, there being a steamer which could render assistance in sight at that time. The firemen were each persuaded to return to their posts with a 'glass of grog', but as each drank his tot the men vowed not to return to the flooded stokehold. In response Captain Wright, his Chief Officer and Chief Engineer together made an inspection and saw the damage for themselves.

Signals of distress were then shown, and the passing vessel, the brand new 4,686 ton **Lakonia**, commissioned only in June that year for Donaldson Brothers of Glasgow, came and stood by. During the night the depth of water in the stokehold increased dramatically and in the morning an unsuccessful attempt was made to pass a towing line to the **Lakonia**. At noon the crew took to the boats and were taken aboard the **Lakonia**. At three that afternoon the **Manchester Enterprise** slid beneath the waves. The crew was eventually landed at Baltimore.

At the subsequent inquiry the story was heard how the ship had foundered in a gale in the North Atlantic on 14 November 1899 outbound to Montreal. The Board of Trade Inquiry was reported in the *Manchester Guardian*, 16 January 1900:

The vessel was acquired in 1898 and placed in dry dock, where £2,000 was spent on her. In October last she was again overhauled and the hull was cleaned and painted at a cost of £400. She was valued at £33,720 and was insured for £32,500, with £2,000 on disbursements, £4,000 on freight and £2,000 for reduction on premiums. Before the vessel sailed from Manchester on her last voyage she had two of her main boilers under repair; it was said that the boilers were thoroughly cleaned and sealed and the bilges were cleaned. The steamer carried 1,800 tons of general cargo and 1,300 tons of bunker coal, 44 hands and 9 cattlemen. After the vessel had taken her cargo and bunker coal on board she proceeded down the Canal. On the way some defects were found in one of the boilers. Everything was put right and the vessel proceeded on her voyage, passing through the locks at Eastham on 5 November.

After leaving the Mersey the vessel encountered heavy weather and on 8 November she was found to have a slight list to starboard. No. 3 hatch was unbattoned and an inspection of the cargo showed that barrels of dye and molasses had shifted. These were restowed with the exception of a few casks which had fallen into one of the coal bunkers. The vessel laboured heavily and although some of the cargo had been restowed she continued to have a list to starboard and this according to the carpenter, increased on 12 November. Nos. 3 and 4 hatches were removed, but the cargo in the holds was found to be secure.

*The Chief Officer reported that when off Innistrahull, in the north of Ireland, the weather was heavy with variable winds. When she left the Mersey the **Manchester Enterprise** drew 20 feet 2 inches of water forward and 24 feet 3 inches aft, and although she was light no great amount of water was shipped. The ship laboured heavily, strong gales being encountered and on 14 November it was reported that the vessel was leaking.*

Descriptions at the Enquiry that the **Manchester Enterprise** 'just leaked badly' and 'could roll even in the Ship Canal' did little for Manchester Liners' image. Crew accusations that the boilers leaked and that the bilges were clogged with debris did little to help. Word even got out that her sister, the **Manchester Trader**, could make better headway in rough weather by going astern than forward, and that she twice took ten days just to get from the Mersey to Queenstown in the south of Ireland! Nevertheless the Inquiry found that the ship foundered due to a leak in the athwartship bunker and that this was no fault of the owners or the manner in which she was equipped. The question as to whether Captain Wright had abandoned ship prematurely fell on the firemen's shoulders. Their refusal to return to the stokeholds, tot of rum or not, meant that there was no steam available for the pumps and the ship started to flood. As for the surviving **Manchester Trader**, well she was a handy sized ship and, as it happened, remained profitable in the fleet for a further thirteen years.

In its first few years of operation, Manchester Liners had proved the viability of the port of Manchester. But it had actually done more, much more. Manchester Liners underpinned the viability of the Canal, so opening the lock gates to a host of new ship owners that wanted a share of the lucrative trade on offer. In so doing they in turn cemented the prosperity of Manchester's hinterland by providing a trade route that had previously been denied to the mill owners and merchants of Lancashire and Cheshire. How much present day Manchester owes to the combined heritage of Manchester Liners and the Manchester Ship Canal Company will never be known but the city should not forget these two key players in wealth creation and the overall prosperity of the region.

Next time you drive across the Thelwall Viaduct and glance down to Latchford Lock you may visualise the red and black funnelled liner rising in the lock, her topmasts lowered inside the lower part of her fore and main masts to reduce her airdraft. And when you next visit the Lowry, glance across the water and you may see the liners once again unloading grain at the Number 2 Elevator at the top of Number 9 Dock. This was not always an attractive waterside residential area but once a thriving industrial port which spawned the Trafford Park industrial complex. The port even attracted Henry Ford to invest locally – 'you can have any colour car you like so long as its black' – but none of this would have happened without Manchester and its Liners.

The success of Manchester Liners lies firmly at the door of Robert Stoker. His careful management and timely expansion enabled a rapid consolidation of the Company ambitions. Besides, he could draw on the assets of the majority shareholder, Furness, Withy & Company, without whose support such rapid expansion would not have been possible.

Stoker no doubt took heed of lessons learned from the foundering of earlier companies dedicated to trade out of Manchester, not least the poorly configured Manchester, Bombay and General Navigation Company which was registered in Manchester by Christopher Furness in 1894. The company was to carry finished cotton goods to India and bring raw cotton and other goods inbound, but Furness had overlooked the strength of the Conference system. He was bought off the route by the Conference members for £11,000 and as a consequence, two of those members, Clan Line and Anchor Line, became established at Manchester from the very early days of the port.

The first sailings on the lucrative Manchester cotton route took place in January 1895, Anchor Line's **Hispania** on the 5th, Clan Line's **Clan Fraser** on the 15th, both to Bombay and the **Clan Drummond** on the 16th to Calcutta. The new Indian service attracted a premium bulk tariff of 20/- per ton, 3/6 more than the existing service to Liverpool, but a significant saving on the combined Liverpool rate plus forwarding by rail to Manchester. These were numbers that the local cotton merchants were quick to exploit, the same kind of numbers, of course, that would also underpin the fortunes of Manchester Liners.

Manchester and its Liners were on a high, enjoying the elevated freight rates that prevailed towards the end of the reign of Victoria. Besides, shipping was at a premium, supporting British military interventions such as the Boer War. Stoker now had his eye out for opportunities to widen the Company horizons and with this in mind orders were placed for a succession of 360 feet long ships designed eventually to succeed the larger 8,000 tonners but primarily targeted at the development of new routes. The stage now was set for the twentieth century.

A NEW INDUSTRIAL LANDSCAPE

The Pomona Pleasure Park, and its celebrated brass band concerts in summer, was overrun by Docks Nos. 1 to 4 above Trafford Bridge. These wharves were designed for the coasting trades with regular calls from Samuel Hough's and Fisher Renwick's steamers on the London service, G & J Burns and M Langlands & Sons steamers on the Glasgow and Belfast services, as well as numerous calls by sailing ships. Dock No. 5 was never built - designed for the stone trade anticipated from North Wales and Cumbria but which never materialised.

Below Trafford Bridge were Docks Nos. 6 to 8 and the turning basin adjacent to the timber clad Trafford Wharf. The main distraction for dockers and sailors alike was Salford Race Course situated adjacent to Dock No. 8 and separated from it only by a low wall. The Race Course was later the site of No. 9 dock equipped at first only on the upstream side leaving large parts of the former Race Course for dockers to rent allotments and, of course, enjoy the inevitable football pitch. Here, many a week's earnings were wagered as a Manchester Liners crew played an international match against a scratch team from some visiting foreign-flag steamer.

Trafford Park, of course, was originally a park featuring a magnificent house, the home of Sir Humphrey de Trafford, with a crystal clear ornamental pond in the magnificent gardens. The park hosted the Manchester Royal Jubilee Exhibition in 1887 and the wonderful glass houses built for the Exhibition were subsequently adopted by the Botanical Society for its annual flower show. Trafford had stipulated that his green and pleasant estate be separated from the adjacent canal between Barton and Mode Wheel by a six foot high red sandstone wall. The remnants of this are still visible upstream from the platform over the Bridgewater Canal at the Barton Swing Aqueduct.

But the wall was a complete waste of effort as Trafford sold out in 1897 to a property developer who rapidly created the world's first industrial estate. The coup was attracting the American Westinghouse Electric Corporation, which set up in 1899 as the British Westinghouse Electric Corporation, and within a few years employed over half the workers on the estate (rebranded Metropolitan Vickers in 1919). Trafford Park also created great wealth and prosperity for Manchester and the north-west, and with it untold degrees of waste and pollution which tax site redevelopment plans in the area dearly to this day.

The remnants of Sir Humphrey de Trafford's wall that once screened his estate from industry with the **Manchester City** (1937) on 13 April 1962.

[Author]

TABLE 1: Ships registered in the name of R B Stoker

Name	Built	Gross tons	Bought and sold
Adria	1864	844	1891 only
Sydenham	1891	2,377	1891-1900
Cynthiana	1891	2,864	1892-1897
May	1890	1,178	1892-1894
Feliciana	1891	2,922	1892-1896
Mandalay	1872	1,915	1892 only
Delhi	1864	2,009	1893 only
Straits of Menai	1894	2,870	1896-1897
Straits of Sunda	1895	2,993	1896-1897
Lady Furness	1895	3,158	1897 only
Knutsford	1903	3,842	1903-1916*

* Transferred seven weeks after delivery to Steamship Knutsford Limited, a company wholly-owned by R B Stoker.

The **Manchester Corporation** (1899) was one of a pair delivered by the Furness Withy Shipyard at Middlesbrough (see page 12).

[John Clarkson]

EDWARDIAN BOOM OR BUST

King Edward succeeded Queen Victoria on the throne in 1901. The new monarch heralded an era of grand ideals. The Edwardians began to shun the prudish values of their predecessors with an air of contentment, perhaps even of arrival, both at home and in their Empire. Lancashire was thriving and its hub, the city of Manchester was alive. The John Rylands Library opened in 1900, the City Corporation took back the leases on the burgeoning tramway system from private operators and began electrifying the system, and Owens College, the Victoria University of Manchester since 1880, continued to maintain its high teaching and academic standards.

The Ship Canal now had a following of liner companies running regular services mainly across the Atlantic to the Americas but also serving the Mediterranean, Africa and beyond. In addition there were many tramp steamers trading to and from Manchester carrying bulk cargoes such as grain inbound and manufactured goods outbound. The Canal Company had its own Canadian agent, Mr R Dawson, and he worked to persuade various carriers to use Manchester. The Manchester Wholesale Provision Trade Association reported that its business had doubled as a result of the new direct links to Canada, the United States and elsewhere.

So pleased was the Ship Canal Company with the trade that had developed that in 1900 it sought compulsory powers to buy the Salford Race Course site to construct No. 9 Dock. In evidence to the House of Lords Select Committee granting the powers was the fact that Manchester Liners alone had brought in 47 ships during the previous nine months. In the event, King Edward opened the new No. 9 Dock in 1905.

A major boost to the reputation of the port occurred in October 1904, as Sir Bosdin Leech reported in the *History of the Manchester Ship Canal*:

*…the **Suffolk**, belonging to the Federal Steam Navigation Company with a beam of 58 feet came up the Canal in nine hours. Her cargo capacity was 10,000 tons deadweight and her gross tonnage 7,313 and net 4,680. This monster of the deep brought a heavy cargo from Australia and with two propellers came up the Canal without a scratch. She had her funnels altered at Eastham, and tied up at Latchford when it was dark. Her voyage has made it clear that big ships can easily come up the Canal in a day.*

A succession of the smaller type ships of the **Manchester Importer** and **Manchester Shipper** mould (Chapter 1) was ordered by Manchester Liners. Starting with the **Manchester Corporation**, which had been commissioned in 1899, all the new builds were equipped with a limited number of twin berth passenger cabins providing either ten or twelve berths in total. The accommodation on the Canadian services was always in demand in the summer months and was a popular alternative to the prestigious main line passenger-mail services offered by Canadian Pacific and others.

The **Manchester Exchange** (1901) was the prototype of a successful class of eight ships designed specifically for the Montreal service.

[Author's collection]

David Burrell takes up the story in his brief history of Manchester Liners:

*The **Manchester Exchange** of 1901, a Furness Withy-built spar decker (i.e. with a shelter deck or 'tween deck rather than a single deck ship) of just over 4,000 tons gross and 360 feet long, proved to be the ideal ship, and between then and 1904 eight sisters were delivered, three from Furness Withy and five from (the) Northumberland (Shipbuilding Company). They were named **Manchester Engineer**, **Manchester Inventor**, **Manchester Market**, **Manchester Spinner**, **Manchester Miller**, **Manchester Port**, **Manchester Merchant** and **Manchester Mariner**. Rather than issue more capital they were partially financed by £300,000 of 4.5% debentures, followed a few years later by a further £100,000 at 5.5%. Both were repaid by the end of 1921.*

The **Manchester Spinner** (1903) in No. 8 Dock at Manchester was another of the **Manchester Exchange** class delivered by the Northumberland Shipbuilding Company.
[Author's collection]

The new tonnage allowed one of the larger capacity ships, the **Manchester Port**, to be sale listed, leaving only her sister **Manchester Merchant** and the **Manchester City** of the larger ships in the fleet. The **Manchester Port** was still a new ship and was seen as an attractive purchase by the Houston Line for their South American route. Renamed **Hydaspes**, she served on this route for the next 29 years until sold in 1930 for demolition.

The **Manchester Merchant** (1904) stayed with the company until sold for breaking up in 1933.
[Author's collection]

Robert Stoker was determined not to be stuck with the vagaries of just one core service and he used his expanded fleet for diversification. The first phase of expansion was a new service to both New Orleans and Galveston which commenced in 1900, with calls at Philadelphia introduced in 1901.

Not forgetting that the Lancashire mills had an insatiable appetite for cotton bales, Stoker decided to load cotton eastbound for Manchester with a view to developing an export trade to the southern states of the US. Stoker also managed to obtain three further ships from the British Maritime Trust, the **Gloriana**, **Italiana** and **Cynthiana**, and these enabled him also to open a new direct service to Boston. Stoker had previously owned the **Cynthiana** between the years 1892 and 1897, before selling her to the British Maritime Trust (see Table 1). In 1901 a joint venture was initiated with Frederick Leyland & Company of Liverpool, a company which later became affiliated with Furness Withy, to serve Philadelphia collaboratively with the Philadelphia & Reading Railroad Company.

The **Manchester Mariner** (1904) was the last of three vessels delivered to the company in the single month of January 1904.

[Author's collection]

The **Manchester Commerce** and Leyland's **Planet Neptune** were responsible for the inaugural sailings while the service settled into a fortnightly departure from Manchester.

Valuable income was earned from Government when various ships were chartered for use as transports in support of the Boer War. The **Manchester Port** was in Government service between October 1899 and November 1902, the **Manchester Merchant** between February 1900 and October 1902, while the **Manchester City** and **Manchester Corporation** both made single trips to the Cape as transports. The **Manchester Port** and **Manchester Merchant** were hugely successful in this role and Government offered to buy them, an offer that was declined by the Liners' Board, keen as it was to receive the charter fees, but keen also to retain the future commercial use of these modern ships.

A rather extraordinary charter was arranged for the **Manchester Shipper** in 1901 as an emigrant ship. Although the Company would shortly be reduced to accepting charters for the carriage of coal in bulk, trading conditions were not yet so poor that it had to resort to the slave trade. In those days, before the loss of the liner **Titanic**, the number of lifeboats required to be carried depended on tonnage not on the number of passengers carried and a special passenger certificate could be obtained provided that additional life jackets were carried. The virtually brand new but moderately paced **Manchester Shipper** was an odd choice, but a desperate need for migrants had arisen in Canada.

Rich iron ore deposits were discovered north of Lake Huron and a railroad was planned to bring the ore to a new iron works to be built at Sault Ste. Marie. The brainchild of the development was American industrialist Frances Clergue, but to see his plans through he needed 2,000 labourers to work in an otherwise sparsely inhabited and generally very cold and barren part of Canada. He was convinced that Scandinavian migrants would suit his need and formed the Franco-Canadian Steamship Company to bring them over with offers of a free passage (a transatlantic berth on a passenger liner was then about 100 Krone, a lot of money against an average working man's weekly wage of just 70 Krone). The 'free passage' actually involved working for Clergue for a minimum of twelve months on arrival for a below par wage.

The newly formed Franco-Canadian shipping company, desperate for passenger tonnage, inspected the **Manchester Shipper** at Montreal and deemed her suitable as a 'passenger liner'. They then set about converting the moveable cattle stalls on the 'tween decks into passenger compartments with four sets of bunked berths two high across each compartment. The **Manchester Shipper** was granted a temporary licence to carry passengers additional to her existing cabin accommodation and set off under the command of Captain Robert Smith for France. Of toilet facilities we know nothing, but visualise the same kind of deck structures with salt water hoses washing faeces overboard via channels on the ship's deck as adopted in World War II aboard the troopships **Queen Mary** and **Queen Elizabeth**.

On embarkation each passenger was given a straw palliasse and a rough wool blanket – veritable magnets for lice. Meals were frugal: a small slice of plain bread and a cup of coffee for breakfast, pea porridge and a slice of ham (small) for lunch and grey water, masquerading as tea, with a biscuit for dinner. Those few with some cash in their pockets could buy wine and extra rations. The first passenger voyage of the *Manchester Shipper* was in June 1901 from Bordeaux via Dunkirk with 235 French emigrants, nine in cabin accommodation. The voyage was blessed with calm weather. She returned to Antwerp, where Captain Smith left ship (ironically to emigrate to Australia) and was succeeded in command by Captain Goldsworthy. At Antwerp the *Manchester Shipper* collected 300 Italian migrant workers and then proceeded to Christiania (now Oslo) in Norway, arriving on 6 April to embark young Norwegian men, each watched anxiously aboard ship by the local population and particularly anxiously by the town's young women. What Captain Goldsworthy had not been told was that there were 512 men wanting 'free passage' and the ship was going to be uncomfortably overcrowded and on board stores at a premium. During the lengthy spectacle of embarkation the Italians started throwing rotten fruit at the assembled crowd which retaliated with snow balls. Animosity continued aboard ship and Italians and Norwegians were duly segregated.

The ship sailed on 8 April, having lain offshore while additional food and water was taken aboard during which time about 50 men had second thoughts about the journey and took flight in local boats. Two days from Halifax Captain Goldsworthy received a collective demand from the Norwegians that they be returned home – two days later he put the Italians ashore at Halifax intending to take the Norwegians on to St John. In the event the men rebelled and fled the squalid conditions aboard ship to create mayhem in the town. Once rounded up they were put on special trains bound for Sault Ste. Marie and other destinations. Apparently few of the men completed their 'contract' with Mr Clergue and most had fled the border into the United States by the end of the summer.

The *Manchester Shipper* made a third and final emigrant run, this time from Le Havre to Halifax. This was during June 1902 when she carried just 233 emigrant workers in greatly relaxed and less confined conditions, two of them paying the price for first class cabin accommodation. Thereafter, cattle stalls aboard the *Manchester Shipper* reverted to bovine use or remained in store at Montreal when not required.

The big steamer *Manchester City* found gainful employment in the River Plate chilled meat trade from 1904. Discussion between Robert Stoker and Ralph Watts Leyland in 1906 led to a joint fortnightly service from Manchester or Glasgow to the River Plate when Frederick Leyland & Company partnered Manchester Liners. This had followed earlier collaboration in a fortnightly service between Manchester and Philadelphia operated by the two companies. The Leyland ships were the *Planet Mercury*, *Planet Venus*, *Planet Mars*, and *Planet Neptune*, each offering 7,500 tons deadweight and a handful of passenger berths. When not occupied on liner services the "Planets" were occupied on tramping duties.

The *Manchester City* was Manchester Liner's main contribution to the service and by 1906 the demand for chilled meat imports was such that the *Manchester City* was converted into the world's largest refrigerated cargo ship. Now with 375,000 cubic feet of chilled capacity she was a large ship to fill with meat imports. Unsurprisingly, the joint venture failed and the service was withdrawn. The *Manchester City*, however, remained in gainful employ in the South American meat trade under charter to the Anglo-Argentine Shipping Company, until that company was no longer able to pay mortgage fees on its other two ships. These two ships became part of a new company, the British and Argentine Steam Navigation Company, which was set up by Furness Withy in 1910 to work alongside the Houlder Line which it then acquired in 1911.

The *Manchester City* continued working the River Plate service from Liverpool. Her partners were the Furness-owned *Guardiana* which was also converted into a reefer and big purpose-built ships, such as Houlder Line's *El Paraguyo* which joined the service in 1912. Houlder's fully refrigerated 'Granges', *Oswestry Grange* of 1902 and her older consorts, tended to work between River Plate ports and Avonmouth.

El Paraguayo (1912) was one of three 8,500 ton coal burning reefers built for Houlder Line which worked alongside the **Manchester City** on the River Plate meat run.

[Author's collection]

Manchester Liners, with its backing from the Furness group, should have thrived with its various services developing support on both sides of the Atlantic in the early years. But one thing the Company could do little about was the shipowners and operators at Liverpool and their Mandelsonian spin doctors who persuaded exporters to turn away from Manchester Liners and return to the older and more established lines working out of the Mersey. Although bulk low value imports such as cereal, deck cargo such as timber and live cattle were assured imports for Manchester Liners, getting full or even near full export loads of machinery, finished textiles and other high cost goods was no easy task. The new company found trading in the early Edwardian era quite taxing despite having significant refrigerated capacity aboard both the **Manchester Corporation** and **Manchester Commerce**, with refrigeration plants being built into other vessels as demand for imported chilled meat and dairy products increased.

But the early safety record of Manchester Liners did little to inspire the faith of the shippers. Incidents such as the **Manchester Port** putting in to St John's, Newfoundland, for repairs on her maiden voyage after hitting an iceberg, the near loss of the **Manchester City** in the Pentland Firth on her delivery voyage and the loss of the **Manchester Enterprise** had done little for the image. But as the century turned the luck of the Company seemingly did not.

The year 1903 was a particularly testing time for the reputation of the new company starting in January with the loss of the **Manchester Merchant** as described in the *Manchester Guardian* 16 January 1903:

*…the **Manchester Merchant**, which was sunk off the Irish coast yesterday apparently in the hope that her complete destruction by fire might be averted, was the largest and finest steamer owned at Manchester. The value of the ship, with her enormous cargo of cotton, grain, turpentine, resin and pitchpine cannot have fallen far short of £250,000, and even if it should be found possible to raise and repair the wreck, an exceptionally heavy loss will fall upon the underwriters. The inflammable nature of the cargo would make it impossible, with the best appliances available shipboard, to extinguish the fire once fairly started. It was fortunate indeed, that in this case, the captain was able to bring the ship into Dingle Bay and get his crew ashore in safety before the flames gained a complete mastery.*

Still the loss of so fine a ship is at best a severe misfortune. The fact that this steamer, after a long and highly successful term of engagement as a Government transport, was bringing her first cargo to her home port in the services of her owners, makes the disaster particularly regrettable and disappointing.

The loss of the **Manchester Market** only a few months later was reported with equal gloom by the *Manchester Guardian* 20 May 1903:

The vessel left Manchester on Friday 24 April with a crew of 40 hands, 6 cattlemen and 2,700 tons of general cargo bound for Philadelphia. She passed the Skerries about 3 am 26 April. The Second Officer, R J Sowden, had charge of the bridge from midnight till 4 am. In rounding the Skerries, knowing or believing that the ship's course had to be altered, he found the Captain, but failing to rouse him from his sleep, took on himself the responsibility of altering course… This in the officer's judgement, should have enabled the ship to clear the Tuskar.

[Next day] the weather was somewhat hazy, with very little wind... on the port bow, at a very short distance, the Tuskar Rock and lighthouse were looming up through the fog. At once the helm was ordered hard a starboard and the telegraph rung for full speed astern and the master called through the speaking tube to come upon the bridge. Receiving no reply the Third Officer was sent to call the master immediately. The master came, and the position had hardly been reported to him when the vessel struck.

At 12.27 the ship hit the outlying rocks on the north west side of the Tuskar and remained fast. She bumped and worked heavily. (Captain Hikins) ordered the boats to be swung out ready for launching and sent the Second Officer to the lighthouse to wire for help; but he returned with the statement that communication with the shore was broken. Twenty-seven of the crew were landed that same evening. The Captain remained on board until 4.30 am on 29 April when he left with the remainder of the crew. The vessel has since become a total wreck.

A reminder of the need for precision navigation in the St Lawrence was made on 3 November 1905 when the six-year-old liner **Bavarian** hit the Wye Rock in the approaches to Montreal. She belonged to the Allan Line of Glasgow which later merged with Canadian Pacific. While all the passengers and crew were safely evacuated from the stricken vessel all hope of salvage was lost when she broke her back and was declared a constructive total loss. The hulk remained in place, advertising the fate of a once proud ship, for the next twelve months before it was removed for demolition near Quebec.

The Allan Line's **Bavarian** (1899) was wrecked on the approach to Montreal on 3 November 1903 - a reminder for precision navigation in the St Lawrence.

[Author's collection]

No dividend was paid on the Ordinary Shares from 1903 onwards, although careful auditing kept the Company solvent. In parallel with Manchester Liners, the Manchester Ship Canal Company was also struggling to maintain a cash flow and its shareholders too were without dividend. Profits were now just nominal and could not be justified given the large capital outlay of the two companies. There were even demands from Manchester Liners' shareholders to withdraw from Manchester completely or to sell vessels to recoup their losses. At this time the thin, but quite attractive, white line around the waist of the ships was painted out as each ship came up for refit – a small, perhaps even mean, saving in annual expenditure against each ship.

Financial crisis in the United States did not help matters. In his annual report to the shareholders, Sir Christopher Furness described 1907 as a disastrous trading year. However, Furness considered that Manchester Liners had not received the input from the merchants and manufacturers of Lancashire which was expected. He threatened that 'if they did not accord to the Liners a larger amount of support, especially with reference to outward cargo, it might even be a serious matter for the Directors to consider whether they should not withdraw their fleet and put them on more remunerative routes'. This warning was welcomed by the shareholders with the words 'hear hear' resounding around the room.

To his credit Robert Stoker kept the Company head-to-wind and was able to offset the difficult trading conditions with a number of profitable charters, so that by 1908 nearly half the fleet was chartered out. One significant, although modest, investment of £20,000 gave the Company an interest in the Furness Withy marine insurance company, so entitling Manchester Liners to concessionary fees, but for the time being at least the Company plodded on, attempting to consolidate its core products and develop shippers' interest in using them.

One embarrassing incident took place in 1908 when the **Manchester Corporation** managed to whitewash the docks at Manchester. Robert Stoker (see references) reports the following:

...a shipment of lard in bulk was being discharged at night into barges alongside and 'by some inexplicable mischance was pumped into Salford Docks'. It is believed that next morning when the engineer responsible saw the Ship Canal white as far as the eye could see, he did not wait to be sacked, but just packed his bags. The lard, we understand, was skimmed off the top, refined and subsequently consumed.

It was only by the end of the decade that the Atlantic trade started to increase and the collective shipping companies again started to look for new tonnage to expand capacity. Indeed, a major problem through much of the 1900s had been too many ships chasing too little prospective cargo on the North Atlantic, so driving freight rates down. An early casualty was the service to the southern US States which was withdrawn in 1909 because of poor freight rates. Comparable rates remained buoyant in other trades, notably to Australia and the Far East. Attractive charter rates were obtained at times from operators such as Watts, Watts & Company who had the **Manchester Miller** on charter under the name **Fulham** between 1905 and 1908, and also with the Furness Withy associate company the Gulf Line. For Manchester Liners part, the first dividend payment on Ordinary Shares was in 1912, some nine years after payment to shareholders had been suspended.

On the North Atlantic, passenger liners had been first to adopt Mr Marconi's new wireless telegraphy system. By 1907 cargo ships were also being equipped, the first being some of the tankers in the Anglo-American Oil Company fleet. Manchester Liners could see the benefit of long-distance telegraphy and, coincident with the upturn in the freight market in 1911, installed the Marconi system aboard the **Manchester City** to determine its worth. As funds became available the system was slowly rolled out to the rest of the fleet, ensuring not only an increased element of safety but also a considerable improvement to the day-to-day management of the fleet.

The year 1911 was the turning point for the Liners. While a number of European shipowners were also trading to Quebec and Montreal, most of these already had transhipment arrangements with the various operators of smaller Canadian flagged ships trading into the Great Lakes. It was logical that Manchester Liners should seek to develop this same trade and a means of doing this was given to it on a plate. A J Henderson described the early history of the Furness Group in an article which first appeared in *Sea Breezes* April 1951:

Through the British Maritime Trust, the company [Furness Withy] purchased in 1911 a substantial holding in the Richlieu & Ontario Navigation Company. Into this had already been merged the Northern Navigation Company and the Niagara Navigation Company, a combination possessing the most extensive cargo and passenger trade on the Great Lakes at that time.

From then onwards goods loaded at Manchester could be trans-shipped at Montreal for Duluth and Port Arthur. This arrangement provided a significant impetus to the traffic now available to Manchester Liners and was a major contribution to the Company's improved prospects. Indeed those prospects improved dramatically over the next few years and by 1913 the Company handled 524,000 tons of goods while its home port had risen to the fourth port in the UK in terms of tonnage. Meanwhile in Canada, Furness Withy had financed further acquisitions and by 1913 had formed Canada Steamships Limited which was then the dominant trader on the Canadian inland waterways.

But the Company still had its mishaps. The **Manchester Commerce** was damaged by contact with ice and started taking in water. She was able to get to St John's, Newfoundand, several days later under her own steam and was subsequently repaired although she was out of service for several months. Captain Everest ordered that her deck cargo of timber, stacked ten feet high on both the forward and after decks, be jettisoned to lighten ship, managed to make St John's, while the vessel was now overdue at Manchester. While in dry dock at St John's the local railroad ran a series of special excursions from the outlying townships to view the ship, which had become something of a curiosity. Meanwhile the fishermen were having a great time off Belle Isle recovering the timber and bringing it home to market!

Large timbers were always a problem during loading and on one occasion a French Canadian winchman was killed when the weight of timber on the derrick buckled the foremast of the **Manchester Inventor**. Lessons were learned rather than blame apportioned at the subsequent Inquiry.

On another occasion the **Manchester Inventor** was trapped in pack ice in hailing distance of the trawler **Halifax 19**. During the night open water appeared near the bigger ship and she was able to get clear. The trawler was never seen or heard from again, presumed squeezed by the ice until sunk with all hands. At about the same time the **Manchester Engineer** was struck by a rogue wave in mid-Atlantic and returned to Manchester with all her port side stove in and battered. Deeply laden, she had been running south before a heavy north-westerly gale and by all accounts was lucky to have survived the incident. Needless to say, contemporary accounts blame a sub-sea storm over ancient Atlantis for creating such a 'tidal wave'!

The **Manchester Civilian** (1913) was the optimum-sized vessel for the Canadian traffic when first commissioned.   [Author's collection]

But by 1912 the Company had money in the bank and ordered two new ships, the first orders since 1904. The new **Manchester Citizen** was delivered by the Northumberland Shipbuilding Company in August 1912 and the **Manchester Civilian** came from Irvine's Shipbuilding and Dry Dock Company at West Hartlepool exactly a year later, both shipbuilders being part of the Furness empire. The **Manchester Civilian** was the slightly larger of the pair being five feet longer at 385 feet and three feet broader in the beam at 52 feet. Nevertheless they were ideal capacity vessels for the North Atlantic trade then on offer. The arrival of the **Manchester Citizen** allowed the now thoroughly outdated **Manchester Trader**, one of the pair of ships bought from Elder Dempster in 1898 when Manchester Liners was created, to be sale listed. She was bought by a Norwegian company and renamed **Ferdinand Melsom** and had two further Norwegian owners before, named **Kaupanger**, she was lost on 13 December 1916 to a torpedo fired by U38, sinking rapidly with a full cargo of Welsh coal in her holds when twenty miles off Cartagena during a voyage from Cardiff to La Spezia.

Sadly, with failing health, Christopher Furness was obliged to withdraw from his business activities and died suddenly in 1912. His place as Chairman of Manchester Liners was logically awarded to Managing Director Robert Stoker. Stoker, who commuted into Manchester from his home in Knutsford, later became MP for the Rusholme Division in south Manchester and was a well-known figure in the city. As war approached the fleet of Manchester Liners Limited stood at fourteen ships which had an aggregate deadweight tonnage of 102,156. Most of the ships were of the smaller 4,000 ton gross design, the exception being the large converted reefer **Manchester City** that remained on the River Plate service. The **Manchester City** was also the oldest ship in the fleet, having been completed in 1898.

Manchester was now a booming port and the industry in its environs had evolved accordingly. A declining cotton industry was being replaced by flour milling and biscuit and breakfast cereal manufacture. Car manufacture at Henry Ford's works, which commenced building Model-Ts in 1911, was doomed to move south to Dagenham in 1931 when the site became too small to allow future expansion. Other port industries had developed in the new Trafford Park Industrial Estate and ranged from chemical manufacture to engineering. The latter included the newly formed Manchester Ship Canal Pontoons and Dry Docks Company which acquired a site just above the uppermost locks at Mode Wheel where a pontoon and two dry docks were built, and a third capable of taking ships up to 8,000 tons was added later. It also had a yard at Ellesmere Port, which had a pontoon capable of lifting 4,000 tons. The

Company was renamed the Manchester Dry Docks Company in 1906. One of its main clients was Manchester Liners Limited whose ships were regularly docked and overhauled by the Company and which was also entrusted with major engine maintenance work.

But despite all this the Manchester Ship Canal Company had not as yet returned a satisfactory dividend to its shareholders, a parallel perhaps with the modern day Channel Tunnel company. The Canal Company Chairman, John Bythell, had a rough few years at the annual general meetings in the 1900s when shareholders attacked the policy of recruiting men not associated with the dock industry into management positions in the Ship Canal Company. In truth this was because no reasonable increment in salary could induce experienced staff with secure jobs in other harbour authorities to join a new company which was not as yet covering its debts. Ironically the fortunes of the Company were improving, in parallel with Manchester Liners, only in the early 1910s, but were set to improve rapidly because of the increased trade that came about during World War I. Happily, from this time onwards, the fortunes of both the Ship Canal Company and its premier client, Manchester Liners Limited, were placed on a more secure footing and the consequent fortunes of both the city and its port hinterland were secured.

Prince Line's **Ocean Prince** (1907) agented in Manchester by Gough & Crosthwaite, high and dry on Manchester Dry Docks' pontoon just above Mode Wheel lock. The Manchester-based part of the Prince Line was acquired by Manchester Liners in 1968.

[Author's collection]

MR ROBERT BURDON STOKER (1859-1919)

Born into a shipowning family in North England in 1859, Robert Burdon Stoker too became a shipowner when he was given his first ship, the 844 gross ton coaster **Adria**, by his father (Table 1). He joined a Liverpool company that operated both sail and steam largely in the American and Canadian trades. He rose through the managerial team at Liverpool to emerge as Manager by the time he was just 23. Hearing of this performance, Christopher Furness, who was then 30, asked the young Stoker to join him as one of his team. Stoker spent an intial three months at the West Hartlepool head office of Furness then went to Newcastle to open a new office to look after the new 'Furness Line' route to America. This service was enjoying the booming export of steel products from the Tees and Tyne as well as from Stockholm and Gothenburg in support of the developing railroad network in America. Homeward cargoes comprised grain, bagged flour, apples and live cattle. Two years later Robert Stoker had built the American line up to a fleet of ten ships with three more added, owned or chartered by year four.

In 1890 Furness asked Stoker to move south to open and run a new office in London as a replacement for a contract agency. By then Stoker had advanced as a shipowner in his own right and in 1891 had the 2,377 ton tramp steamer *Sydenham* built as a successor to the *Adria* which was then sold for demolition. Other ships owned by Stoker are listed in Chapter 1, Table 1, although he only retained the *Sydenham* from 1897 onwards. When Furness Withy & Company was formed in 1891, Robert Stoker was appointed to the Board as Ship Director under Furness' chairmanship. In addition Furness' godson Frederick Lewis, later Sir Frederick Lewis, was sent to train in London under Stoker, and by all accounts the protégé showed an immediate flair for maritime business.

On 5 May 1898 the Prospectus of Manchester Liners Limited was announced, with a total issueable capital of £1 million. At the invitation of majority shareholder and Chairman of the new company, Sir Christopher Furness, Stoker resigned from the Board of Furness Withy to become the first Managing Director of Manchester Liners Limited. Stoker presided over the early rapid growth of the Company then had to carefully manage his Company through a decade of deflated freight rates on the North Atlantic. On the untimely death of Furness in 1912, Stoker was elected as Chairman of Manchester Liners and was succeeded as Managing Director by former Company Secretary Mr F E Vaughan.

In 1903 Stoker, who had sold the last of his family owned ships, the *Sydenham*, in 1900, ordered and took delivery of a new tramp steamer aptly named after the town he lived in, the *Knutsford*. The *Knutsford* was built for him by Robert Stephenson & Co on the Tyne and was delivered in July. A few weeks later, however, Stoker opted to register her under a limited liability trading company, Steamship Knutsford Limited. The *Knutsford* was crewed and managed by Manchester Liners. She was kept in the Canadian coastal coal trade for much of her career and her port agents throughout were Furness Withy. Her master, Captain Butler, was awarded the coveted Gold Cane by the Harbour Master at Montreal when the *Knutsford* was the first steamer up the ice-blocked St Lawrence one year, an achievement Manchester Liners' ships had not yet attained. Stoker sold the *Knutsford* in 1913 to Roth Brothers of London but repossessed her seven months later for default of payment. He finally sold the ship at considerable profit in 1916, but her new owners promptly resold her. She was later sunk by gunfire on passage to Baltimore.

For much of his tenure as Chairman of Manchester Liners, Robert Stoker steered his Company through the dark years of the Great War. In March 1918 Robert Stoker was elected Member of Parliament unopposed as the Coalition Conservative candidate for Manchester South, the previous incumbent having been killed in action. With the reorganisation of the constituencies later in the year, Stoker became the first MP for the new Rusholme Constituency. Sadly, shortly afterwards, he was taken ill and died only six years after he was elevated to Chairman of the Manchester Liners' board. Robert Stoker was succeeded in the Chair by none other than Sir Frederick Lewis, while at the same time Robert Stoker's son Kenneth became a Director of Manchester Liners. Kenneth Stoker was later also to become Managing Director (in 1932) and subsequently Chairman (in 1959). In turn, Kenneth Stoker's son Rob, named after his grandfather, Robert Burdon Stoker, also took his turn as Managing Director and later Chairman of the Board of Manchester Liners.

Managing Directors		Chairmen	
Robert B Stoker	1898-1912	Sir Christopher Furness	1898-1912
Sir Frederick Lewis	1912-1919	Robert B Stoker	1912-1919
F E Vaughan	1919-1932	Sir Frederick Lewis,	
Kenneth Stoker	1932-1965	Lord Essendon of Essendon	1919-1944
Rob B Stoker	1965-1968	Sir Ernest Murrant	1944-1959
WAL [Tony] Roberts	1968-1986	Kenneth Stoker	1959-1968
		Rob B Stoker	1968-1979
		Tony Roberts	1979-1986

CHAPTER 3

THE GREAT WAR – THE U-BOAT AND THE MINE

The Chairman of the Manchester Ship Canal Company, Mr Bythell, worried about the onset of war and the likely impact it would have on the business prospects of the Canal. He was convinced that war would take his traffic away as ships turned round at Liverpool or Glasgow without having time to venture up to Manchester. As a consequence he ordered that all non-essential company personnel, many of the clerks, runners and other support staff, be placed on short working hours to conserve his resources. But he had overlooked the massive increase in demand for merchant shipping in times of war when the military needed additional transport to support its combat forces. In actual fact, traffic on the Canal all but doubled overnight and staff were returned to normal hours while others were rostered for overtime. The increased number of pilotage and towage fees as well as the basic harbour dues lined the company's pockets ready for hard times that may lie ahead.

Manchester Liners, in similar vein, found that freight rates rose favourably as there was more cargo on offer than ships available to carry it. The value of merchant ships escalated as the war progressed so that the capital value of the 'Liners increased rather than decreased throughout the war years. Not only that, but favourable charter rates were also available from Government - from a business perspective the early war years were lucrative.

Some particularly awful new offensive hazards for mariners were introduced to this war. These were the submarine, the torpedo and the mine. But it was also the war in which hundreds of thousands of men faced each other in trenches across a line which moved to and fro as battles over small parcels of land were won and lost.

One of the first things that happened was that many of the Lake steamers of Canada Steamship Lines were sent down the St Lawrence and across to the UK to help the war effort. On arrival they were placed under the management of majority shareholder Furness Withy. The condition of the vessels was of concern and the cost of getting them seaworthy was a bone of contention between Furness Withy and Canada Steamship Lines. An immediate consequence was the sale of shares in Canada Steamship by Furness Withy in an attempt to distance itself from what it now realised was a grossly undercapitalised and cash strapped outfit. In the event the company only survived with a massive injection of money post-war from US investors. As for the ships at war on the high seas – they were a liability and excuses were found to retrench them, one by one, to the Canadian inland waters although a couple stayed on international service to the end.

As for Manchester Liners, it took just two days following Britain's declaration of war against Germany for the **Manchester Engineer** and **Manchester Importer** to be requisitioned as transports. Both ships had been lying at Manchester lightly loaded and on 17 and 21 August respectively they commenced cross-channel ferry duties between Southampton and Le Havre in support of the defence of the Western Front. While the **Manchester Importer** remained on the Channel throughout the war, the **Manchester Engineer** forsook her ferry role in June 1915 and was then transferred to the American supply route to Britain.

The **Manchester Commerce** was the first ML war casualty and the first British merchant ship to be lost to a mine. She had sailed light from Manchester bound for the St Lawrence when at 0445 hours on the morning of 27 October, just as morning coffee was being delivered to the watch on the bridge, she struck a mine on the starboard bow. Her position was off Tory Island in a channel that the Admiralty had previously declared to be safe from mines. Chief Officer Caldwell briefed the master, Captain Payne, who had been off duty, and the pair set about launching the lifeboats. Although it was a dull autumn morning there was a sea running and it was no easy task. The Chief's lifeboat was got away but the **Manchester Commerce** was taking water so rapidly that the launch crew of the second lifeboat were overwhelmed as the ship sank, just seven minutes after striking the mine. The master and thirteen of his crew lost their lives that morning.

The ***Manchester Importer*** (1899) was requisitioned as a transport in the early days of the war.

[John Clarkson]

R B Stoker in his account of Manchester Liners wrote:

*The first intimation of this loss was apparently when the Fleetwood fishing boat **City of London** put into Carnlough Bay, Co. Antrim, and reported her rescue of 30 survivors. The disaster occurred on one of the routes fixed by the Admiralty which had been communicated by secret instructions to shipmasters and shipowners a very short time previously. The speed and facility with which the route was mined proved that the German Secret Service Agents had discovered the Admiralty's instructions and had been instrumental in the dispatch of a ship wearing neutral colours to lay the minefield.*

The minelayer was the converted passenger liner **Berlin**, requisitioned from the North German Lloyd Line and illegally flying the Swedish flag. The liner survived the war and was taken as a war prize to become the White Star Line's **Arabic** in 1921. The **Manchester Commerce** was ultimately replaced by a new ship to be named **Manchester Hero** on her completion in 1916. She was bought on the stocks from Furness Withy's Northumberland Shipbuilding Company in December 1914, having been ordered by the Austro-Hungarian shipping company Lloyd Austriaco of Trieste.

During the summer of 1914 the **Manchester Civilian** was modified as a collier. Her 'tween decks were partly removed and cross boards were inserted for bulk carriage of coal. Listed as 'Collier No. 414' she was dispatched, along with the chartered **Manchester Miller**, fully laden with steam coal under Manchester Liners masters, Captain G Spencer in charge of the **Manchester Civilian** and Captain Robertson aboard the **Manchester Miller**, on passage to the South Atlantic. Unlike the **Manchester Civilian**, the **Manchester Miller** had not been specially converted as a collier and later resumed general cargo duties. A long way from No. 9 Dock, the two ships were lying in the sheltered waters off Port Stanley in the Falkland Islands by early December.

On 7 December the battle cruisers HMS **Invincible** and HMS **Inflexible** came alongside the two Manchester Liners and started to transfer fuel to the battle cruisers' stoke holds. The cruisers HMS **Glasgow**, HMS **Kent** and HMS **Cornwall** were anchored nearby. This dirty and dusty operation was rudely interrupted when Vice Admiral Sir Doveton Sturdee learnt that Vice Admiral Graf von Spee's five raiders, the armoured cruisers **Scharnhorst** and **Gneisenau** and the light cruisers **Nürnberg**, **Dresden** and **Leipzig** were approaching. Believing the Falkland Islands to be undefended von Spee planned to take Port Stanley with his two big ships **Scharnhorst** and **Gneisenau** but was appalled to see the masts of so many enemy ships emerge over the headland as he approached in the dull light of the morning of 8 December.

The crews of the **Manchester Civilian** and **Manchester Miller** had a front row seat as the two German cruisers fled to the south east, unaware that none of the anchored British ships had steam up. Within two hours Sturdee's flotilla was in pursuit and von Spee found that he was outranged and outgunned, losing the **Scharnhorst** with all hands, including von Spee, at 1645 hours and **Gneisenau** with only a few survivors going down at 1800 hours. Only the **Dresden** survived. Many years later when Sir Doveton Sturdee was on an official visit to Manchester Docks he stood and saluted the **Manchester Civilian** which was alongside, declaring that she had been an essential and honourable part of the campaign.

On 12 November 1915 the **Manchester Merchant** was able to effect rescue of 15 men from the Brazilian barque **Storeng** which was foundering in a gale in the North Atlantic. For their action the master, Captain E W C Beggs, and his Chief Officer, H Brown, were thanked at a reception given by the Lord Mayor of Manchester and the Liverpool Shipwreck and Humane Society. The incident offered a reminder that there were two enemies, the sea and the German navy.

The **Manchester Merchant** (1904), armed and wearing dazzle camouflage.
[Author's collection]

Also in 1915, a joint wartime service to Baltimore was commenced under the title Furness-Johnstone-Manchester Liners. Various ships were used on the route depending on availability of tonnage within the consortium. Vessels loaded at Manchester or Avonmouth.

The **Manchester Engineer** was lost to a torpedo, fired by submarine U44 which had been patrolling the St George's Channel, on only her third voyage to the United States following her stint on the Channel supplying the British Expeditionary Force. The incident took place on her return journey to Manchester off Waterford on 27 March 1916, so close to her destination, losing not only a sound ship but also a full inventory of American stores that were so desperately needed to support the war effort. Happily Manchester Liners survived the remainder of the year without further incident.

The **Manchester Hero** was commissioned from her Tyneside builders in early January. Shortly after she was commissioned, she was shelled by a submarine off the west coast of Ireland. Under Captain Perry she was able to outpace her pursuer with volunteer stokers whipping her up to a speed reported to be as high as 16 knots. Comments were also made that the **Manchester Hero** (or could it have been her stokers?) never quite recovered from this effort and that she struggled thereafter to make even her design speed of just 11 knots.

The **Manchester Hero** (1916) was delivered during the war.
[John Clarkson]

Compensation for losses allowed purchase of replacement ships outwith the Furness Withy empire, some of which were given the same names as ships lost earlier in an attempt to confuse the enemy's reporting of sightings and losses. In March a slow 9 knot steamer, the **Auchenblae**, was purchased from Glasgow owners. The target speed for fleet members was 10 to 11 knots at that time. Nevertheless, she was given the name **Manchester Trader**, her former namesake having been sold before the war. But both the **Manchester Commerce**, bought from Liverpool owners State Steamship Company, and the **Manchester Engineer** which was bought from the Treasury Steamship Company also of Liverpool in May, were named after earlier war losses. Both vessels were lost to U-Boat torpedo attacks in 1917, the **Manchester Commerce** on passage to Gibraltar and the **Manchester Engineer** on a voyage to St Nazaire after surviving a brush with **U28** on 8 June 1917 when north-east of Vardö.

Within quick succession early in 1917 the **Manchester Inventor** and then the **Manchester Citizen** were lost while carrying out their normal commercial transatlantic duties. Both ships were sunk inbound to Manchester from St John off Fastnet, the one captured by U57 and sunk by gunfire on 18 January and the other torpedoed by U70 on 26 April. On 4 June the **Manchester Trader** was in the Mediterranean eight miles off the Italian coast when she came upon U-Boat U65 on the surface. The British merchantman, like all others, was poorly equipped, with one gun forward and one aft, but managed to put up a creditable gunfight before she was sunk by shellfire. One crew member was taken prisoner by the U-Boat while all but one of the remainder of the crew managed to get safely to shore. For their action the master, Captain Frederick Struss, who had joined Manchester Liners in 1907, and his Chief Engineer, W R Strobo, each received the Distinguished Service Cross.

The very next day, 5 June, the **Manchester Miller** was sunk with the loss of eight lives. She had been inbound from Philadelphia when she was hit by a torpedo delivered by U66. Once again confusion was attempted as the second-hand purchase of the Liverpool-registered **Celtic King** adopted the name **Manchester Inventor** just two months after her former namesake had been lost to gunfire.

The **Manchester Miller** (1903) at the head of No.6 Dock in Manchester in more peaceful times.

[Author's collection]

The 'new' **Manchester Inventor** was allocated to the Russian convoys and arrived at Archangel on 4 June 1917. On the return she was loaded with flax and routed around the top of Scotland and bound in convoy for Belfast. On 30 July at a point north-east of Muckle Flugga she was sunk by gunfire by U94. There was, however, no confusion over the identity of the **Manchester Inventor** as the captain of the U-Boat knew the original **Manchester Inventor** from his many trips in peace time as a merchant ship master which took him to the same berths in Montreal as the Manchester Liners.

On the same day that the **Manchester Inventor** was arriving at Archangel, the **Manchester Port** was in mid-Atlantic heading for the St Lawrence when a U-Boat surfaced nearby ready to attack. Some very quick action followed with some surprisingly accurate firing from the **Manchester Port** which succeeded in making the submarine submerge again. Like the **Manchester Civilian**, the **Manchester Port** had been used as a fleet collier for much of the war voyaging to Egypt, the Caribbean, Falkland Islands and even Callao on the Pacific coast of Peru.

In December 1917, Captain Groth brought the **Manchester Mariner** fully loaded with a cargo of steam coal into Falmouth with damage caused by a mine. The vessel was granted permission to proceed to Leghorn (now called Livorno) on the Italian peninsula with her cargo destined for the Royal Navy, her master being told 'to nurse her'. The final loss of the war was the **Manchester Spinner** which was torpedoed in the Mediterranean on 22 January 1918. She had been returning home from Salonika with a cargo of sugar, having been on Government service since 1916. In May the **Manchester Importer** received a hit by a torpedo but was able to continue to her destination for discharge and repairs.

Two new ships were added to the fleet in 1918 in the final days of war. They had been ordered from Irvine's yard at West Hartlepool back in 1914 but their completion was not seen as a war priority. The two ships were almost identical sisters, the first to be launched being the **Manchester Brigade** in February, followed by the **Manchester Division** in June, with both delivered just as the war ended.

The war delayed the delivery of the **Manchester Brigade** (1918) by nearly three years and she was commissioned at the end of hostilities.

[John Clarkson]

The new **Manchester Division** did see some action, however, and on her delivery voyage south to Plymouth to join a convoy, Captain E W C Beggs was able to ram and sink a German U-Boat manoeuvring on the surface off Flamborough Head. The U-Boat's steel radio aerial was later found wrapped around the propeller of the **Manchester Division**. Captain Beggs had first gone to sea in 1881 aboard the iron barque **Pole Star**, and came to Manchester Liners in 1903 to take charge of the brand new **Manchester Miller**.

Throughout the hostilities the big steamer **Manchester City** remained on the chilled meat import route to the River Plate. The mainstays of the Company's commercial services between Manchester and Canada were the **Manchester Corporation**, **Manchester Shipper**, **Manchester Merchant** and **Manchester Exchange**.

At the time of the Armistice on the eleventh hour of the eleventh day of the eleventh month of 1918, peace once again reigned in Europe. Manchester Liners had lost ten ships during the hostilities, eight of them in the years 1917 and 1918, when the U-Boats had developed team work skills and started to hunt in packs. These figures reflect the overall allied losses of 13 million tons gross during the war of which over 9 million tons representing 4,500 ships was lost in the years 1917/1918. The eight losses of Manchester Liners in these years released Government compensation of a little over £1.12 million, ironically leaving the Company better resourced at the end of the war than it had been at the start.

At the start of the war the Company owned and operated fifteen ships. In November 1918 it had twelve vessels (Table 2) including the brand new **Manchester Brigade** and **Manchester Division**, and it also had cash in the bank. The Company shareholders were at last content, having received substantive 25% dividends on the shareholdings for the previous three years.

Manchester and its people had come through the war years none the worse to face a new and, for the time being, less threatening world. The First Brigade of the Manchester Regiment had returned from India at the start of the war to join the rest of the Regiment on the Western Front. Manchester's own regiment conducted a brave war with moments of outright gallantry shown, for example, at the withdrawal at Mons by men who at that time must have been thoroughly tired and worn out. Manchester and its Liners had conducted themselves well and were now set to pick up the threads of 'Civvy Street'. The Great War was at last over and men swore that never again would the world be engulfed in such war and carefully took measures to ensure that the German military could not be rebuilt and put back on the offensive. History was yet to tell us how inadequate these precautionary measures would turn out to be.

The **Manchester Division** (1918) was the sister to the **Manchester Brigade**. This bow view shows her in the River Mersey and approaching Eastham with topmasts already lowered.

[Author's collection]

Sadly we have neither the date nor the location of this photograph of the **Manchester Division** but it does allow us to see her from the stern and with all masts.

[Bernard McCall collection]

COMMODORE FREDERICK DOUGLAS STRUSS DSC, OBE (1882-1955)

Frederick Struss was born in the parish of St Peters, Liverpool, on 30 June 1882, the son of Henry and Rebecca Struss. Frederick first went to sea as an apprentice aboard the four-masted barque *Seafarer*. He rapidly worked his way through the ranks until 1907 he received his master's certificate. Shortly afterwards he was appointed Chief Officer with Manchester Liners.

During the Great War he was in command of the *Manchester Trader* when she was sunk by U65 on 4 June 1917 on passage to Algiers in ballast. Her single high angle 12-pounder gun designed for anti-aircraft work was put to good use before the ship was finally captured only after a running fight lasting over six hours and she was sunk by gunfire. Sadly, one crew member was killed in the incident and another taken prisoner, the remainder including Captain Struss and his Chief Engineer, both of whom were later awarded the DSC for their part in the incident, were set free in the ship's boats. They were picked up six hours later.

Captain Struss later succeeded Philip Linton as Commodore of the fleet in 1940 at which point Frederick Struss moved from command of the *Manchester Port* to the newest ship which was the *Manchester Progress*. In May 1940 it was the Commodore's duty to commission the latest fleet member and he then took command of the *Manchester Merchant* at the Blythswood yard on the Clyde. Just two years later the *Manchester Merchant* was torpedoed 200 miles off Newfoundland on the morning of 25 February 1943 on passage from Manchester to Halifax in convoy ON166. The ship staggered and took on water at an alarming rate before the boats could be got away: 29 crew and six gunners were lost. The master, unconscious and clinging to a plank, plus 27 crew members and four surviving gunners, were picked up from icy seas and landed at St Johns. Frederick Struss survived immersion in the icy sea with only his plank and a buoyancy jacket. Again he was honoured for his service, this time receiving the OBE.

The Commodore subsequently commissioned the *Manchester Shipper*, the *Manchester Regiment* and then the next *Manchester Merchant*, before standing by the *Manchester Spinner* fitting out at Birkenhead in 1952. Throughout his long career he had an impeccable accident free record and was greatly respected for his navigation skills, particularly in the days when the patent log and the sextant were the only tools available.

Very much of the old school, complete with square rig certificates, Captain Struss stood no nonsense, forbade his officers any social contact with passengers and generally commanded with strict dispassionate authority. Although never popular with his officers, he always held their great respect. For all this, he was a quiet and short-spoken man and while he could be quite gruff with strangers he was cordial to the extreme with friends. Quiet spoken or not, the Commodore, just like his predecessor Commodore Linton, was a colourful character whose roots lay firmly in the age of sail but who progressed with ease to the steam turbine age and navigational aids such as radar.

The last voyage for Commodore Struss saw him arrive at Montreal on 30 March 1954 to take the Montreal Gold Headed Cane - a fitting award for a man who had spent his entire working life at sea. He bought the *Manchester Spinner* alongside without the aid of tugs as they were still frozen in at their winter hide-out in a corner of the dock. On arrival back in Manchester the Commodore was told that he was to be retired. The master's suite was cleared as the former Commodore packed his bags ready to focus on gardening and listening to music at his Sale home. Sadly, this idyll was not to last and he died peacefully at home on 20 June 1955, survived by his widow, son and daughter.

MORE TRIPLE EXPANSION ENGINES, A TURBINE STEAMER AND HALF A MOTOR SHIP

On many a still winter's day, Manchester found itself suspended beneath a thick, sooty black cloud – the Manchester smog. Under certain weather conditions the smog could settle over the city for days. The particulate soot and suspended coal smoke carried in the smog had already turned the welcoming golden yellow millstone grit building stone of the Cathedral into a forbidding black and quite ordinary looking church. The Town Hall was similarly converted into a monstrous black Victorian monument. The smog turned the starched white collars of the office workers grey by lunch time and black by tea, and many faces needed a wash on coming inside. So thick was the cloud on occasion that looking up from the street even the black lines of the tram wires were concealed. The good, long suffering citizens of Manchester coughed and spluttered their way through the working day before going home to sit by their coal fires, and the once abundant sparrows stood on their perches, and they too coughed!

Coal was very much the driving force of the period. Robert Stoker, of course, had sold his steamer **Knutsford** at the start of the war, and her replacement in the Canadian coastal coal trade was the former Admiralty collier **Manchester Civilian**. Although not exclusively used in the bulk coal trade, she spent much of the immediate postwar period distributing coal from the Sydney Mines jetty on Cape Breton Island to a variety of coastal destinations and ports along the St Lawrence. But unlike the **Knutsford**, coal for the ship's furnaces did not come from the hold. When the old **Knutsford** had been on charter carrying coal between Australia and Shanghai before the war, her Chief Engineer would have 20 tons of coal lifted from the hold each night, and doused the remaining cargo with 20 tons of sea water to keep the vessel on her load line! Her master was a cousin of Robert Stoker, but it was the cousin that was able to retire early on his 'earnings' not the owner!

Much to the relief of the other crews, Manchester Liners was able to deploy the rest of the fleet within the core transatlantic product – for the moment. But the many vessels that had carried bulk coal never quite got rid of all the coal dust – it was found in cabins and lockers, cracks and crannies, on the steel ribs that lined the sides of the holds and a host of other hiding places for years to come.

Sadly in 1919 at the height of an influenza epidemic, Robert Stoker died after a brief illness. His passing was mourned by his surviving family and by Manchester Liners. This was the man who had overseen the birth of the Company and carefully developed his fleet to suit his trade. He then had to nurture his Company through the depressed North Atlantic freight rates that prevailed in the 1900s before taking it safely and profitably through the dark years of the war. Sir Frederick Lewis was appointed as the succeeding Chairman, stepping up from the role of Managing Director. Freddy, as he was known in his younger days, had been sent by Christopher Furness to learn the trade under Robert Stoker when he was still with Furness Withy.

One of the first changes that the new management brought about was the formation of a limited liability subsidiary company under the name Manchester Ocean Services Limited. This new private company was registered on 1 April 1920 with an authorised capital of £1.5 million. It had the same directors as Manchester Liners. The company objectives were 'to carry on the business of shipowners, act as ship and insurance brokers, to manage shipping property, to be carriers by land and sea, owners of barges and providers of lighterage'. Into this was transferred the ownership of three of the oldest ships, all dating from 1904: the **Manchester Mariner**, **Manchester Merchant** and **Manchester Port**. This manoeuvre brought £48,228 into the parent Company's account in 1921 while repaying the debt on instalment by way of charter fees. The financial benefit of this arrangement to Manchester Liners is not recorded, but it is likely to have assisted with offsetting part of its overall tax burden.

But the main reason for the new holding company was that it, and not Manchester Liners, was in discussion with Furness Withy regarding an option for three large turbine steamers. These were planned as part of a group of six to be built at the Furness Shipbuilding Company at Haverton Hill on the Tees. Minutes of Manchester Liners' Board record considerable caution - that the Board did not want the new turbine technology failing them, that it was worried about upscaling from 6,000 tonners to 8,000 tonners and finally it worried over how many ships to buy. Despite business being comparatively brisk in the immediate post-war years, pressure from Furness Withy to order three ships was not easy to allay. The idea of working the risk through a separate holding company thus provided that vital element of insurance needed by the Manchester Liners' Board. If all failed, Manchester Ocean Services could be allowed into receivership without any significant impact on Manchester Liners, or so was the theory. The three old ships were the sprats for the mackerel, and each would be sold as the new turbine steamers were commissioned.

Charles Parsons' turbines had first been taken commercially to sea by the Merchant Navy in 1901 on the Clyde excursion steamer **King Edward**, to be followed shortly thereafter by the fast cross-channel ships of the South Eastern & Chatham Railway. Experiments with turbines aboard cargo ships in 1910 with the **Vespasian** had proved the technology a success for larger vessels of this type (the **Vespasian** had been built as Prince Line's **Eastern Prince** in 1887). Cairns Noble & Company of Newcastle had followed the trials with great interest and ordered the turbine steamer **Cairnross**, which was delivered in 1912, for its Newcastle and Leith to Montreal or winter St John services. Sadly a war loss, she was replaced in 1921 by a new turbine-powered **Cairnross**. Furness Withy watched this development like a hawk and clearly wanted part of the action.

In 1913 Cairns Noble bought the **Vespasian** with a view to installing her turbines in a new hull. The war, of course, intervened. Manchester Liners was keen enough to try the new turbine technology with all its perceived efficiencies and consequent enhanced deadweight, but it had to have a large enough ship in which to try it. It was also faced with the dilemma of having to take three ships in the first instance rather than just one as a trial and Manchester Ocean Services provided a safety net for doing just that.

Canadian Pacific's **Bothwell** (1918) was built as the **War Beryl** and was one of a number of wartime standard ships placed on commercial service in competition with ML after the Great War.

[Author's collection]

While Manchester Liners was planning its fleet replacements, other companies were buying up the war-time standard ships built at the behest of Government. The Doxford-built **War Beryl**, with a handy deadweight of 11,095 tons, for example, was one of several that Canadian Pacific acquired. Renamed **Bothwell**, she ran from Liverpool to Quebec and Montreal in summer and St John in winter in direct competition with ML.

The brief post-war boom allowed Manchester Liners to reinstate all its pre-war services, that to New Orleans in 1920, while the Baltimore service now included a call at Norfolk in Virginia. Demand was such that the Company was running out of ships, having reached the end of the war with three less than it had in 1914. The turbine steamers could not be on stream until at least 1922 and interim tonnage was desperately needed. The Company was offered two of the smaller Furness Withy owned units. These were the **Start Point**, which had been completed at Sunderland in 1916 for the Norfolk & North American Steam Shipping Company, and the **Grampian Range**, a product of Irvine's yard in 1917 and delivered originally to the Neptune Steam Navigation Company. Furness had acquired the Norfolk & North American in 1910, so giving it access to Philadelphia, and the Neptune company in 1906. In May 1921 the **Start Point** adopted the name **Manchester Producer** and the **Grampian Range** became the **Manchester Spinner**.

The **Manchester Producer** (1916) at Montreal. She was formerly the **Start Point** owned by the Norfolk & North American Steam Shipping Company.

[Ray Carter with permission of Neil Carter]

Late in 1921 the market ebbed, the post-war boom came to an end and the beginnings of a minor recession started to take hold. Rather than having too few ships Manchester Liners now found it had too many and quickly set about backing out of the option for the big turbine steamers. It was allowed to abandon orders for two of the three ships but was obliged to take the **Manchester Regiment** which had already been launched and was fitting out on the Tees. Of the class of six near identical ships, the other two orders were absorbed into the Furness Withy empire, making a total of three to Furness Withy rather than just one, and one to both Neptune and Norfolk and North America.

Four of the steamers eventually found their way into the Harrison Line following a downturn in trade in the North Atlantic and temporary service for three of them on the Prince Line route to South Africa. The **Politician**, formerly the **London Merchant**, became a source of mirth after she was wrecked in a storm at Eriskay Sound in February 1941. The local highlanders were quick to discover she was carrying a luxury cargo destined for the United States as payment towards war materials, and even quicker to discover the whereabouts of the large consignment of whisky in the 'tween decks. Much of this was in hiding places ashore long before the Customs arrived on the scene. The whole episode was the source for the post-war novel *Whisky Galore* by Compton McKenzie and the subsequent film that was distributed in 1949.

The **Manchester Regiment** was a complete diversion for Manchester Liners. Not only was she turbine driven, whereas the remainder of the fleet had always been driven by reciprocating triple expansion engines, but she had capacious holds (11,572 tons deadweight) that had to be filled on each voyage if a profit was to be assured.

The new ship was delivered in August 1922, but she was perceived as such a prestigious purchase that rather than being put under the ownership of Manchester Ocean Services she rightfully belonged under Manchester Liner's own banner. The **Manchester Regiment** quickly set up the record passage between Liverpool Bar and Quebec for the Company in just seven days and nine hours. The Manchester Regiment was invited to sponsor the ship and this it did with all the pomp and circumstance that befits such an event.

Prestigious she certainly was, but at what cost? Her capital outlay amounted to £458,600, a significant part of which was the cost of her engines. Such was the cost of the ship herself that when depreciation was added to running costs she was a poor second to the smaller old fashioned triple expansion steamers. Manchester Liners slowly realised that its fingers had been burnt and it would be quite a while before another turbine steamer was ordered. Indeed it was not long before the **Manchester Regiment** was moored in Salford for protracted periods, there being insufficient cargo on offer to warrant her putting to sea.

The **Manchester Regiment** did have a plus side. She was the flagship of the fleet, she was big, she was impressive and she was fast. She also managed to be the first ship up the St Lawrence in 1925 when Captain Foale was presented by the Montreal Harbour Authority with the first of the ten Gold Headed Canes that would be awarded to Manchester Liners skippers over the years. But impressive though she was, it is suggested by a number of analysts that throughout her career the **Manchester Regiment** never turned a profit.

The ***Manchester Regiment*** (1922) in the St Lawrence. She was the first turbine steamer in the fleet.

[Author's collection]

This same Captain Foale had been told on one voyage to be especially polite to an important lady passenger. One night at dinner this lady was having trouble getting any salt out of the salt cellar. The Captain came to her rescue 'Let me help you, madam' and picking up the salt cellar he valiantly blew down its top!

Silver-plate salt and pepper pots engraved 'Manchester Liners Ltd' by Walker & Hall, Sheffield, pre-1923 - which begs two questions: Just how many times could this cruet have passed through Barton Bridge? And secondly, could the salt pot ... could it conceivably be the one blown down by Captain Foale for his important lady passenger?

[Author's collection]

Coincident with the delivery of the ***Manchester Regiment***, headquarters staff moved into their brand new, purpose built, offices between St Ann's Church and Cross Street. Manchester Liners House, as it was christened at the opening, was pure luxury compared with the cramped quarters that had been home in rented office space in Deansgate for the previous twenty odd years. Manchester Liners House was designed by Harry Fairhurst who decided that the new building should be proudly clad in Portland Stone. Manchester Liners House was to remain the base for the company until it outgrew even this in the late 1960s. An attraction to passers by were the two shop windows on the ground floor in which builder's models of Company ships were always on display. As time went on the older models tended to migrate up Cross Street to feature in the magnificent marble floored entrance hallway of the city Town Hall. Manchester was indeed proud of its Manchester Liners.

The newly-acquired **Manchester Spinner** was causing problems. Good for just 10 knots, she was hard pressed to cope with the adverse 'winter North Atlantic' weather and declining traffic soon made her redundant. Rather than sell the vessel, she was put onto the Canadian coastal charter market alongside the **Manchester Civilian**, immediately getting coal dust into her veins and that of her crew. Respite for the pair came in 1923 when they were both chartered for humanitarian relief work carrying American supplies to Japan following the Yokohama earthquake. Both ships made several voyages to Japan before returning to Cape Breton Island for further punishment. That same year another Manchester City moved into its new Maine Road stadium in Moss Side, while United, which had been at Old Trafford since 1910, was slumbering in the Second Division, having been relegated the previous year.

The Furness Pacific Line started business through the Panama Canal (which had opened in 1914) to the western seaboard ports of America and Canada in 1921. Manchester and London were the principal UK ports for the service, and Manchester Liners was appointed agent for the service at Manchester. The first Manchester departure was taken by the **Mongolian Prince**, a vessel that - had she been loading at Manchester for her owners - would otherwise have been agented by Gough & Crosthwaite from their Oxford Street offices. Prince Line had been acquired by Furness during the war in 1916, but retained its own Manchester agent. David Burrell in his history of Furness Withy wrote:

*Various other Prince Line Ships were employed on the [new Pacific] service and were joined in 1923 by the new **Dominion Miller** with her pioneer Doxford diesel. The earlier **Northwestern Miller** and **Southwestern Miller** followed together with ships such as **London Shipper**, **London Merchant** and **London Importer**. With a decision to introduce a new nomenclature having the Pacific prefix, **Dominion Miller** was renamed **Pacific Commerce** and continued to serve with new ships [all with Pacific names] specially designed for the service.*

Furness Pacific's **London Importer** (1923) was a regular visitor to Manchester where Manchester Liners acted as agent.

[Author's collection]

The reduced freight rates from 1922 onwards signed the death knell for Manchester Liners' service to New Orleans which was withdrawn. The Philadelphia service was reduced to fortnightly and then only monthly departures were offered. Conditions did not improve and in 1924 the Chairman's report to the shareholders explained that while regular services had been maintained it had not been found possible to find gainful employment for the whole fleet with several ships laid up at Manchester for extensive periods. ML did, however, have a £0.5 million reserve fund, a sum equal to the total of the Ordinary Share Capital, and investment of this money had helped maintain a profit for the year 1923/1924 of £64,660. In perspective even this sum was poor especially compared with the rich pickings of the war years and the short-lived post-war boom:

Year	*Profit*		*Year*	*Profit*
1913/14	£47,493		1918/19	£195,039
1914/15	£186,692		1919/20	£163,635
1915/16	£174,177		1920/21	£68,906
1916/17	£111,618		1921/22	£64,660
1917/18	£137,899			

The second generation Furness steamer **Pacific Exporter** (1928) approaching Eastham lock.

[John Clarkson]

But despite the poor trading conditions the fleet was ageing and new tonnage was essential to keep Manchester Liners in business, the more so should business actually start to improve. The new ships were the triple expansion engined **Manchester Commerce** and **Manchester Citizen** built by the Furness Shipbuilding Company at Haverton Hill at a cost of £268,000 the pair. Nearly half the cost of the two ships was funded by mortgages guaranteed by the Treasury under the Trade Facilities Act. The design speed of the ships was 13 knots which allowed a small upgrade in voyage times compared with the earlier steamers which maintained service at anything between 11 and 12 knots (the **Manchester Regiment** excepted).

ABOVE: The **Manchester Commerce** (1925) was delivered by the Furness Shipyard at Haverton Hill.

[Max Cooper]

OPPOSITE: A twin berth passenger 'State Room' aboard the **Manchester Commerce** (1925).

[Author's collection]

The pair was the last of the triple expansion engined ships to be built for the company and all subsequent vessels were either turbine driven or motor ships. Their boilers, however, were innovative, being designed either for coal burning or oil burning. It was the latter option that was adopted, wisely providing the sisters with independence from the forthcoming protracted strike action by the nation's coal miners during 1926. Strangely the company reverted to coal fired boilers for another 18 years until the **Manchester Shipper** was commissioned in 1943.

A glowing technical account of the new **Manchester Commerce** was published in the *Manchester Guardian* 26 March 1925:

The hold and 'tween decks have been specially arranged clear of obstructions to allow for the safe and rapid handling of cargo. Steel grain divisions and wooden shifting boards in the way of hatches are provided in the holds and lower 'tween decks for the carriage of grain cargoes. The bridge and upper 'tween decks are fitted out for the transportation of 500 head of fat cattle. Numbers 2 and 3 cellular double bottom tanks, the midships cross bunker and fuel tanks, port and starboard, in the engine room, are arranged for the carriage of oil fuel. Special heating arrangements are provided for heating the oil fuel in cold weather.

New ships and reduced sailings allowed the elderly steamers **Manchester Port** and **Manchester Mariner**, belonging to Manchester Ocean Services, and the **Manchester Exchange**, which was still registered under the parent company, to be disposed of during 1925. Manchester Ocean Services retained just one asset, the equally venerable **Manchester Merchant**.

The year 1926 did not start well for Manchester Liners. The **Manchester Merchant**, lying innocently alongside at Philadelphia, was struck by the steamer **Margaret** causing extensive damage to both ships. Then in February Manchester Liners hit the headlines for all the wrong reasons. The **Manchester Producer**, under Captain G M Mitchell, was eastbound in mid-Atlantic when she lost her rudder. Not in itself a tragedy but with 386 cattle stowed in stalls on deck and in the 'tween decks, life soon became uncomfortable as the ship heaved helplessly to the Atlantic swell. Help was soon at hand and the smaller steamer **Comino** was able to get a line aboard and keep the bigger ship head to wind. She was able to pass her charge over to the larger and more powerful **Menominee**, but little headway could be made with the line parting on a couple of occasions. As the weather eased, first the **Mongolian Prince**, coming up from Panama, and then the **London Commerce** on the Furness' Canadian run took over the tow and after 17 days the stranded Manchester Liner was towed into the Azores.

The **Manchester Citizen** (1925), sister to the **Manchester Commerce**.

[John Clarkson]

But what a mess. Feedstock for the animals had long since run out and grain had to be brought up from the hold as the only substitute. Those animals housed on deck, in stalls that had been damaged and soaked in icy sea water, were of necessity sacrificed in an attempt to feed and care for those in the 'tween decks. When the ship reached Fayal, only 253 animals remained alive, and many of those required urgent veterinary attention. The press had a field day, and Manchester Liners were associated with anything but compassion for quite a while. But despite the attention the incident received, it was a further twelve years before the carriage of live cattle across the Atlantic was finally banned.

The **Manchester Civilian** made a plea for help from her grimy coal runs up the St Lawrence when in May 1926 she took the ground. For nearly three months she lay on an exposed foreshore in the Gulf of St Lawrence while her cargo of iron, lying on top of coal, was offloaded into a smaller vessel. Much of the remaining cargo of coal and coke deep in the holds was jettisoned to further lighten ship. Nearly three months after the **Manchester Civilian** had run aground, she was floated off and then steamed cautiously to Quebec. The recovery was overseen throughout by the Halifax Shipyard's salvage vessel **Reindeer I**.

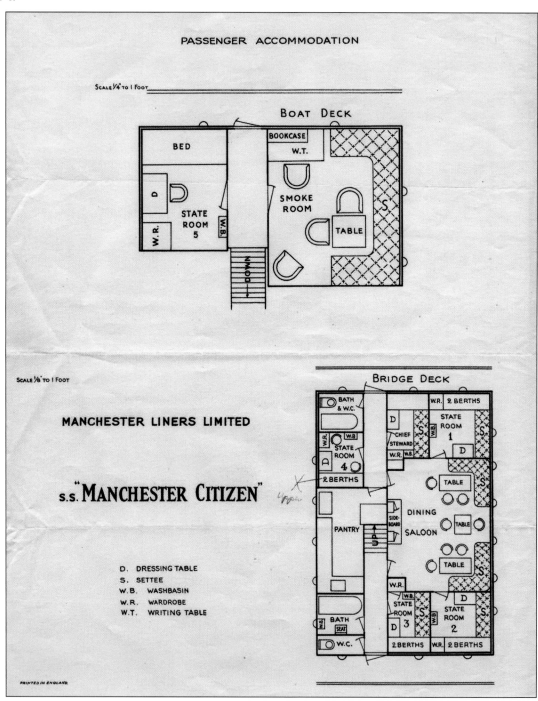

Passenger accommodation for the **Manchester Citizen** showing the dining saloon and four twin berth state rooms on the Bridge Deck, one single state room and the smoking room on the Boat Deck.

[Author's collection]

But 1926 was not a good year for anybody in the UK. This was the year of the General Strike, the workers with diminishing disposable incomes, now at their last tether. The coal miners decided to stay out and the subsequent coal strike wrought havoc with industry and with coal-fired shipping in particular. Manchester Liners were able to get through this mess by bunkering in Canada. To make matters worse live cattle shipments from Canada to the UK were embargoed as a result of foot and mouth disease involving many Canadian cattle ranches, following an initial outbreak in 1924. This move starved Manchester Liners of much of its traditional homeward cargo income. The 1920s were by no means easy years for Britain, and they were particularly hard on Manchester Liners.

In 1927 the **Manchester Importer** was sold after giving her owners 28 years of service. She had been only the fifth ship to join the newly formed Manchester Liners then in its second year of trading. But the big reefer **Manchester City** was still plying her way down to the South Atlantic and into the River Plate to load frozen beef and she was exactly the same age as the **Manchester Importer**. She too had served her owners well, maintaining the River Plate service and running also to the St Lawrence, as required, to load Canadian beef and dairy products. The **Manchester City** had paid for herself several times over and the Manchester Liners' Board were faced with a quandary. Their ship was getting expensive to run, her machinery was outdated and inefficient and basically she needed replacing. The problem was that the economy of scale on the long run down to Argentina meant that nothing smaller than 9,000 tons could be contemplated - but at what cost?

While Manchester Liners was reluctant to commit itself to a new build for the River Plate service, an opportunity arose which offered a good compromise. The British & Argentine Steam Navigation Company, which was managed by Furness-owned Houlder Brothers, was building a large new refrigerated motor ship at the Fairfield Shipbuilding & Engineering Company yard at Govan. She was 431 feet long and 64.5 feet broad, dimensions that prevented her from ever using the Manchester Ship Canal. Her engines were twin six-cylinder Sulzer oil engines driving separate shafts and built under licence at Fairfield and these were to provide a service speed of over 14 knots. The Manchester Liners Board was able to negotiate a half share in the new ship which cost a total of £412,000 to complete. Manchester Liners parted with a cheque for £206,000 and became the proud owners of half a motor ship.

The new ship was given the traditional British & Argentine company name **El Argentino** and set off southwards from her Liverpool base for the first time in April 1928. On her next inbound trip the **Manchester City** was unloaded and destored then sailed light ship northabout Scotland to Norway for delivery to the Stavanger Shipbreaking Company. The **El Argentino** generated a handsome return to Manchester Liners against its capital investment. The ship was crewed by Houlder Brothers with certificated diesel engineers in charge of the engine department. Although Manchester Liners now owned a part share in a motor ship, the company would not embark on building one for its own services for a further 28 years. It did, however, warm to steam turbine machinery with new builds commencing with the **Manchester Port** class in 1935.

ML held a half share with the British & Argentine Steam Navigation Company of the refrigerated meat carrier **El Argentino** (1928).

[John Clarkson]

A month after the **Manchester City** departed for the last time the **Manchester Corporation**, also dating from 1899, was sold for demolition and sailed from Manchester to Thomas Ward's yard at Barrow. So by the end of the 1920s the only pre-Great War built ships in the Manchester Liners' fleet were the **Manchester Shipper** and **Manchester Civilian** although the **Manchester Merchant** was managed by Manchester Liners but still registered under the ownership of Manchester Ocean Services Limited. One 'new' ship joined up when the **Rexmore** was bought from Furness Withy at the favourable price of just £55,000 and adopted the name **Manchester Exporter**. She had been completed in 1918 for the Johnston Line for use on the service from Liverpool to the Black Sea and Mediterranean and was a useful stop-gap until trade recovered sufficiently to warrant further investment in new ships.

Manchester Liners was again in the headlines at the end of the decade. In December 1929 the **Manchester Regiment** answered a distress call from the steamer **Volumnia**, owned by Gow Harrison & Company of Glasgow, which was sinking in a gale in mid-Atlantic. While the American tanker **Saco** pumped oil on the seas to windward, a boat from the **Manchester Regiment** made two hazardous trips to the stricken **Volumnia**, a big ship of 5,608 gross tons, and rescued the entire crew of 45 men.

Robert Stoker (junior) again:

*The **Manchester Regiment** [Captain Philip Linton] steamed 160 miles through a gale to reach the sinking Glasgow steamer **Volumnia**. A lifeboat was launched manned by Second Officer W H Downing, Third Officer E W Espley, Bo'son J Bromage, Seamen Stringer, Kearns and Manins and Mr R P Zeigler, a passenger. The crew of 45 doomed men were saved by 'remarkable seamanship, skill and courage of the master, officers and crew of the **Manchester Regiment**'. On return home the King awarded the Silver Medal for Gallantry in Saving Life at Sea to the officers and crew of the lifeboat, and the Lord Mayor of Manchester presented a silver salver from the Board of Trade to Captain Linton.*

The presentation by the Lord Mayor was covered by the *Manchester Guardian* 14 December 1929:

*At the Manchester Town Hall yesterday the Lord Mayor, Councillor Barclay Hide, held a reception in honour of Captain Linton and the officers and crew of the **Manchester Regiment**. The Lord Mayor called particular attention to the difficulty that had been experienced in selecting a crew for the **Manchester Regiment**'s lifeboat, because officers and men without exception were anxious not to be left out. He made appreciative references to the selection of one of the passengers, Mr Ziegler; to the heroism of the Second Officer, Mr Downing, who carried on in charge of the lifeboat although in the launching of it he had lost a finger joint; and finally to the wise and masterful seamanship of Captain Linton.*

The **Manchester Exporter** (1918), formerly the **Rexmore**, joined the fleet in 1929 when she was bought from Furness Withy.

[John Clarkson]

The Manchester Ship Canal Company added its own praise: 'this achievement which had stirred the imagination of the world would ever be a source of inspiration to the whole nation, and of singular pride to the home port of Manchester'.

Although Manchester Liners had rightly been very cautious in the 1920s, particularly with investment in new ships, it had invested elsewhere. It increased its shareholding in Furness Withy's insurance company, now named the Economic Insurance Company, and it had taken £100,000 worth of shares in the Furness-owned Neptune Steam Navigation Company. Of course, it had also invested in its own new headquarters building off St Ann's Square and occupied newly-acquired accommodation for the shore gang supervisors situated at the head of No 8 Dock.

The depressed freight rates on the North Atlantic had slowed the ambitions of the Company but not destroyed them. Manchester Liners had successfully delivered its core product and had come through a period of difficult trading conditions. Like many other commercial ventures at the end of the 1920s it looked forward to better things to come. Alas, as we well know, the 1920s were merely the introduction to the Depression and much worse was yet to come.

The **Manchester Regiment** (1922) locking out of Mode Wheel, a tight fit. The pole masts will have been raised after passing the Irlam railway viaduct to clear loose stays ready for cargo handling.

[Author's collection]

WHAT'S IN A NAME?

With the word MANCHESTER emblazoned on port and starboard bows and written twice on the stern, Manchester Liners' ships were clearly proud of their home port. All of the liners, apart from chartered vessels, were registered at Manchester. Although nearly all the Company-owned ships carried the 'Manchester' nomenclature there were several separate phases of names. Of these the most distinctive were the new container ships introduced with the *Manchester Challenge*-class from 1968. Indeed the three box boat sisters *Manchester Challenge*, *Manchester Courage* and *Manchester Concorde* heralded a bold new era with names that reflected the container revolution and, of course, began wtih 'C' for container. Subsequent names reflected an increasing element of hope, the *Manchester Miller* being converted to carry containers in 1970 under the new name of *Manchester Quest*, while other new names during the Company's twilight years seemed to cross hope with anxiety as in *Manchester Crusade*, *Manchester Zeal* and *Manchester Vigour*.

The majority class of name was the 'occupational' name: *Manchester Trader*, *Manchester Importer*, *Manchester Merchant*, *Manchester Shipper*, *Manchester Engineer*, *Manchester Inventor*, etc. There were also the institutional names *Manchester Market*, *Manchester Corporation* and *Manchester Exchange* and the activity names such as *Manchester Progress*, *Manchester Commerce*, *Manchester Enterprise*, the latter being the Company's very first ship. And there were place names - or were there? The *Manchester Port* is clearly a place but what was the *Manchester City*? It appears that the 1937-built *Manchester City* was not a celebration of the City of Manchester at all but rather a celebration of the fortunes of the football club which had just become the champions of the First Division. That there was never a 'Manchester United' probably reflects a leaning towards Protestantism on the part of the Board, supporting Manchester City with its traditional Protestant following rather than United, which was the Catholic club. R B Stoker in his history of the Company states 'The year 1937 saw the new *Manchester City*, a tribute to her predecessor and, incidentally to the successful local football team..."

There was also the military class of name which appeared first during World War I with the *Manchester Hero* in 1916 and the *Manchester Brigade* and *Manchester Division* two years later. The most famous of this class was undoubtedly the *Manchester Regiment* which was delivered in 1922 and her proud namesake which entered the fleet after World War II in 1947. Both ships were adopted by the Manchester Regiment. There was also one *Manchester Civilian* which was delivered in 1913.

The name *Manchester Citizen* was used twice. The more obvious name 'The Manchester Man', the title of the book by the celebrated author Mrs George Limmaeus Banks, was not used although it was suggested by the author of this book in the 1960s, but rejected as being too similar to *Manchester Mariner* in RT exchanges. It was nevertheless listed as a potential name for future use but once the *Manchester Mariner* was retired from the fleet the Company had already turned to its hope and anxiety nomenclature.

The remaining class of name was the specials given to the purpose-designed ships for pioneering a new service into the Great Lakes in the early 1950s prior to the opening of the St Lawrence Seaway in 1959. Two little ships were ordered from Cammell Laird at Birkenhead and ventured up the Welland Canal to the lake ports in 1952 with the highly appropriate names *Manchester Pioneer* and *Manchester Explorer*. They were joined by the second-hand *Manchester Prospector* to satisfy demand on the new service and in due course by the engines aft twins *Manchester Venture* and *Manchester Vanguard*. In anticipation of the opening of the St Lawrence Seaway the larger, though still modest sized for Manchester Liners, *Manchester Fame* and *Manchester Faith* were commissioned. It is interesting that the celebrated names *Manchester Vanguard* and *Manchester Venture* were used again, the second time around for two large container ships which were commissioned in 1977 for the charter market in an attempt to keep up with the economy of scale offered by bigger ships. They were designed to run from Liverpool, as they were too large to enter the Ship Canal to access their own home port.

So what is in a name? The traditional occupational and institutional names reflected industry in the hinterland of the Port of Manchester while the military names reflected times of conflict. The special names used for the ships which opened up the Great Lakes service and the 'C'-class names of the first container ships all carried the excitement and challenge of the day. Sadly, the final phases of 'hope' and 'hope and anxiety' preceded the disappearance of the Company within the burgeoning ship owning interests of C Y Tung of Hong Kong in 1980, along with the rest of the Furness Withy Group.

CHAPTER 5

THE 1930s – THE PIONEER FAST CARGO LINERS

The depressed freight rates of the 1920s on the North Atlantic rolled on into the early 1930s. The good news was that the embargo on live cattle shipments from Canada was lifted in 1930; the bad news was that the Salford Foreign Cattle Lairage was destined to close and that ML would have to transfer allegiance to the Birkenhead Lairage. More ship disposals were desirable as departure schedules were reduced in intensity to match the cargo on offer. This allowed the oldest ship in the fleet, the thirty years old **Manchester Shipper**, to be disposed of and sold for demolition in July 1930. But the worst was still to come. As if the Wall Street Crash of October 1929 had not upset freight rates enough, a further devastating impact on North Atlantic trade saw pound sterling fall in value from US $5 to US $3.5 during 1931. The ripple effect of the original crash hit global trade to such an extent that during the worst of the recession one third of the British mercantile marine was laid up with canvas covers over funnel tops, the crews destined for the ranks of the unemployed.

Having unloaded Canadian cattle at the Birkenhead Lairage, the **Manchester Brigade** (1918) heads for Eastham inbound to Manchester.

[Author's collection]

The impact on Manchester Liners was less than it might have been. The Company had already largely retrenched from the highly competitive Philadelphia service and had reduced its core product to Canadian ports to a bare minimum. The **Manchester Spinner**, which had retained her shelter deck throughout her collier work, had been brought home from the Canadian coal charters. By 1931 the **Manchester Civilian** also finally gave up the Canadian coastal coal work on which earnings no longer covered the costs of the ship. Both the **Manchester Spinner** and **Manchester Civilian** spent much of 1932 idle, joining the **Manchester Regiment** which had now seen little active service for a number of years. The following year the **Manchester Civilian** was sold for further service under the Greek flag. During the early autumn the **Manchester Merchant** was also sold, but this time the scrap merchant's price was adequate compensation.

Managing Director Mr F E Vaughan died in 1932 and was succeeded by Robert Stoker's son Kenneth. Kenneth Stoker had been a Director of the Company for the previous thirteen years. Also appointed in 1932 was a Mr Robert (Rob) Stoker (junior), the 18-year-old son of the new MD, who joined the Dock Office. Robert and his grandfather both shared the same name of Robert Burdon Stoker, and Rob Stoker would one day follow in both father's and grandfather's footsteps and rise to the role of Managing Director, eventually also succeeding father Kenneth as Chairman. In the meantime the trade needed to be learned and the practicalities of that trade were nowhere better evident than at the Dock Office at No. 8 Dock, recession or not.

The **Manchester Regiment** was involved in a search for survivors following the loss of Ropner Shipping Company's **Saxilby** in mid-Atlantic as reported by the *Manchester Guardian* 17 November 1933:

*Little hope is out for the safety of the crew of the British steamer **Saxilby**, who took to their boats in a fierce gale in the Atlantic about 300 miles off the Irish coast. Three of the vessels searching for the men - the Cunard liner **Berengaria**, the British steamer **Manchester Regiment** and the Dutch steamer **Boschdijk** – notified in wireless messages that they have abandoned the search and are proceeding on their voyages... At Manchester Captain Mitchell's message read 'Sighted no wreckage. Afraid impossible boats to survive weather.'*

Through 1933 and into 1934 the world started to trade again and the consumer slowly returned to the idea of having a disposable income with some, albeit modest, purchasing power. It was a slow and painstaking recovery, the more so with the Canadian and American transport network, in which trust was regained and orders once again placed overseas for shipment of goods and commodities back home. While Manchester Liners had been able to continue providing its basic Canadian service with seasonal connections arranged from Montreal into the Great Lakes, the Furness Withy companies on the North Atlantic had not fared so well. The Cairn Line had been able to keep its two newer turbine steamers, the **Cairnesk** and **Cairnglen**, on the service between north-east England and Canada, but its other three ships had been mothballed for the duration.

David Burrell in his Furness history reports other consequences:

By 1934, however, the North Atlantic routes had been decimated and all that remained was the Furness-Warren Line from Liverpool to Boston, Halifax and St John. This led to the decision in 1934 to merge the three Liverpool companies, Neptune, Warren and Johnston into a combined Johnston Warren Lines. It was to be 1939 before the needs of war led to the reopening of the New York service.

Manchester Liners had invested heavily in the Neptune Steam Navigation Company in the 1920s. The 'Liners Board had been keen to see cash sitting in the bank converted into a more rewarding asset at a time when new building was deemed unwise (Chapter 4). This shareholding was automatically converted from Neptune to Johnston Warren shares at the time of the merger.

The address from Chairman Frederick Lewis, Lord Essendon of Essendon from 1932, to his shareholders at the 36th Annual General Meeting of Manchester Liners, held in October 1934, included the telling passage:

During the year under review we have maintained our regular services. Actually we have increased our Canadian sailings and have offered shippers practically an unbroken weekly service throughout the year. We have been compelled, however, through the absence of profitable employment, to lay up certain steamers for varying periods.

Nevertheless, the Manchester Liners' Board, under the guidance of Lord Essendon, watched patiently, waiting for the moment it might be prudent to start to renew its fleet. In the meantime it had started discussion with the Blythswood Shipbuilding Company at Scotstoun on the Clyde regarding the design of a new pioneer class of fast shelterdeck cargo liner.

Furness Withy had sold off its shipbuilding interests in the late 1910s, although the Furness family retained interest in the Furness Shipyard at Haverton Hill and a number of orders continued to be placed with old friends at Irvine's Shipbuilding & Dry Docks Company. The Northumberland Shipbuilding Company, which also used to build for Manchester Liners, had been sold in 1918 into a consortium that included amongst others the Blythswood company. Thus by the mid-1930s Manchester Liners was free to talk to any shipyard regarding new orders. Besides, the initial days when 43% of the 'Liners shares were held by Furness Withy were long gone (although Furness Withy does buy back into Manchester Liners in due course) as various share issues had significantly eroded the Furness dominance. As it happened, the partnership between Manchester and Blythswood, now seen as a friend of the Furness family through the Northumberland connection, was to be fruitful and profitable for both parties.

The new design was to be a big ship in anticipation of the mid-1930s upturn in trade which would allow Manchester Liners to steal a march on its competitors. The 'Manamax' design would enjoy the perceived optimum dimensions of the Ship Canal locks, but was, nevertheless, some 30 feet shorter in length than the **Manchester Regiment** and a couple of feet narrower than her. Unlike her predecessors, apart from the **Manchester Regiment**, the new design incorporated triple steam turbine units connected to a single shaft and boilers fuelled by coal but with automatic stokers which required special pulverised fuel. Such fuel was available on both sides of the Atlantic but would limit the vessel ever being chartered out for use in the Far East or the Pacific where pulverised coal was not readily available at the bunkering wharves. But the economic savings of automatic coal fuelling overcame any such reservations and were clearly seen as a better investment than fuel oil as already used in the 1925-built **Manchester Commerce** and **Manchester Citizen**.

The design speed of the prototype was 13.5 knots, just 1 knot less than the **Manchester Regiment** which had proved to be too expensive a ship to turn a profit. Emphasis was placed on carrying cattle, special ventilation for fresh fruit and particular attention was paid to the comfort of twelve passengers, whilst the crew's quarters were a great advance over earlier ships.

Modern in every way, the new design was developed to a stage that a contract for £129,000 could be placed during 1934 for one ship known as Yard No. 38, with an option for two further vessels subject to sea trials with the prototype vessel. Yard No. 38 was given the name **Manchester Port** when she was launched into the Clyde at the end of July 1935. Three months later the new ship completed fitting out and trials and sailed south for the Mersey and Manchester. In her early years she was mainly employed in the live cattle trade with stalls built on the exposed main deck as well as the 'tween deck. Live cattle were brought in from Canada to the lairage at Birkenhead before the ship came up to Manchester to unload her deep holds where grain and other bulk cargoes were stowed. The prototype pioneer fast cargo ship was deemed a success and an order was placed for a second ship with Blythswood.

The **Manchester Port** (1935), seen in the late 1940s, was the first of a hugely successful class of eight ships built by the Blythswood yard at Scotstoun for ML.

[John Clarkson]

The *Manchester Guardian* 13 August 1936 excitedly talked about the new class of ship and described the second vessel building at Blythswood as follows:

...will have a single screw and be fitted with Scotch boilers employing self firing furnaces automatically fed. Here is one of the alterations between the old and new ships, for each boiler will be fed by three instead of four furnaces. The main machinery is being supplied by David Rowan & Company of Glasgow and consists of one set of single reduction geared turbines of Parson's type, the boilers being 16 feet in diameter and 12 feet in length and operating under forced draught, having a steam pressure of 225 lb per square inch. A coal burning ship, she is designed to give a speed when fully loaded of 13.5 knots.

Double state room aboard the **Manchester Port.**

[Author's collection]

Social room aboard the **Manchester Port.**

[Author's collection]

The **Manchester City** (1937) in her dotage on Lake Ontario wearing Great Lakes green livery.

[Fred Sankoff]

The second ship was named **Manchester City** in honour of the 1936/37 season First Division championship winning football club - before Manchester City F C were relegated at the end of the very next season. She was launched on 23 June 1937 by Miss Betty Killock of Bowden, a niece of Managing Director Kenneth Stoker. Outwardly the **Manchester City** was the same as the **Manchester Port**, except that the wooden bridge structure of the **Manchester Port** was replaced by a steel plated bridge, giving the new ship a more modern, but less traditional, appearance.

The main difference between the two ships was that the **Manchester Port** measured 422 feet between perpendiculars and the newer **Manchester City** 431 feet, the latter being a few inches more beamy than her sister. The propelling machinery was the same with another set of turbines made by David Rowan & Company in Glasgow providing 3,800 shaft horse power. When delivered to Manchester in August an identical sister to the **Manchester City** was already rising from the slipway at Scotstoun with delivery planned for late 1938.

The two new vessels allowed the wartime-built **Manchester Hero** to be sale listed in the spring of 1937. She was bought by the B & S Shipping Company of Barry and given the name **St Winifred**. Within the year the **St Winifred** was lying at Alicante where she was bombed by the Spanish Nationalists. Unable to leave port, the hapless steamer was again bombed, a victim of a foreign civil war. Several months later a tow was arranged and the vessel was taken to Marseilles where she was declared a constructive total loss. But just as some car insurance write-offs tend to be bought and patched up by the mechanics under the railway arches, so the **St Winifred** suddenly reappeared on the register, this time under the Italian flag. As the **Capo Vita**, the former **Manchester Hero** was sunk in the Mediterranean early in 1941 by a British submarine. The old Mancunian obliged by taking her cargo of munitions to the bottom.

The **Manchester Hero** (1916), seen inbound at Eastham, was sold in 1937.

[John Clarkson]

But in 1937 there was also the curious incident of the **Manchester Regiment** and Clan Line's **Clan Mackenzie**. So curious an incident was it that the case became a focus of attention for quite a few years whenever conversation turned to compass adjustments in shipping circles. The large and now rather stately **Manchester Regiment** was sailing at 'slow' down the Mersey approach channel to a point near the Bar, as was customary, to manoeuvre for compass adjustments.

The **Manchester Regiment** (1922), outbound at Eastham before the forward goal post was strengthened, was involved in a collision in the Mersey while compass adjusting.

[John Clarkson]

David Burrell takes up the story:

*The **Manchester Regiment** was in the news when, on 23 October 1937, she was in collision with the **Clan Mackenzie** (6,554 tons gross and dating from 1917). Sailing from Liverpool for East London, the Clan Liner overtook the **Manchester Regiment** which was flying the flags JI, the signal that she was adjusting compasses. The **Clan Mackenzie** was rammed on the port side and had to be beached. Later refloated she was declared a total loss, sold and broken up at Troon in 1938. The case went to court where the judge considered which rule of the road should apply, and decided fault lay **Manchester Regiment** 80% and **Clan Mackenzie** 20%.*

When the **Clan Mackenzie** was brought into Gladstone Dock, much of the bridge structure was missing and the whole ship was covered in a thin layer of brown mud. The **Manchester Regiment** was barely damaged save for a few buckled plates forward.

The next of the new class of turbine steamer was named **Manchester Progress** on her launch from the Blythswood yard on 28 June 1938. She too was fitted out especially for the carriage of live cattle and fruit, complete, as were the others, with twelve passenger berths in single and twin berth cabins. She was delivered in September for a contract price of £190,000, nearly 50% greater than the cost of the first ship in the series delivered only three years earlier, a reflection of post-depression inflation.

On passage from her builders on the Clyde, on 18 September 1938, to load cargo for her maiden voyage, the **Manchester Progress** (1938) enters Barton locks assisted by the paddle tug **Old Trafford** (1907).

[A R Prince]

The **Manchester Progress** (1938) emerging through the Barton bridges, inbound on 9 April 1963.

[Author]

The arrival of the **Manchester Progress** in the North Atlantic trade coincided almost exactly with the banning of the import of live animals from the Americas for slaughter in the UK. The cattle stalls destined for the **Manchester Progress** lay unused in a warehouse in Quebec, and were soon joined by the timber from her consorts as they each returned to the Canadian port. In the 39 years Manchester Liners had been involved in the cattle trade, the Company's ships had carried over 2.6 million animals of which just 746 had died at sea. Of these, 133 animals had been lost aboard the **Manchester Producer** when she lost her rudder in mid-Atlantic in February 1926 (Chapter 4).

The Company half-share in the big frozen meat carrier **El Argentino** was sold late in 1937, ending the 'Liners involvement in the River Plate service. Her registered ownership had been changed from the British & Argentine Steam Navigation Company to Furness Withy & Company in 1934 as part of an overall consolidation of the River Plate meat trade, but Manchester Liner's investment remained unchanged. There were a number of reasons for the disposal, not least that Vestey's Blue Star Line had earlier been invited into the Conference effectively providing over capacity at a time of weak freight rates. The former British & Argentine Steam Navigation Company had already been ceded to Houlder Brothers (Furness, Houlder Argentine Lines), who in any case retained management of the big motor-ship which continued in trade on her designated route between Buenos Aires and Liverpool. The Chairman's report at the 40th Annual General Meeting in October 1938 explained the Board's main reasons for disposing of its interest in the **El Argentino**:

*This interest was acquired some ten years ago with the intention of continuing our participation in the South American refrigerated meat trade following the breaking up of the original **Manchester City**, which vessel had been specially fitted out for the trade many years earlier. Since then, however, with the advent of quotas and restrictions on the one hand and the necessity of new tonnage for our own services on the other...to take advantage of an opportunity that occurred to dispose of this investment.*

One more ship was sold in 1939, the new turbine steamers having more than proved their worth. In May 1939 ML announced that orders for two further ships placed again at the Blythswood yard at Scotstoun would both qualify for the new Government shipbuilding subsidies. The first of the pair was expected for delivery early in 1940 and the total contract price was £400,000.

The political climate in Europe was deteriorating rapidly as Neville Chamberlain, with his characteristic starched upright shirt collars, treated the dictators Hitler and Mussolini to a 'policy of appeasement'. When it was clear to the Board of Trade that appeasement was unlikely to deter the will of the German and Italian leaders, they, along with the Admiralty, set about planning for outright war. For its part, the Board of Trade created the Merchant Ship Reserve under the Board of Trade Shipping Assistance Bill (1939), buying suitable second-hand tonnage with which to service the needs of increased military movements. Ten ships were purchased by September 1939. One of the purchases was the **Manchester Producer**, dating from 1921, and she exchanged her Manchester crew for a Glasgow crew when she was placed under the management of P Henderson & Company in August 1939. Ten days after war was declared she was given the standard BOT name **Botwey**. Her sale price was just £17,500.

The **Manchester Producer** (1921), in the Mersey with the Johnston Warren Line tugs **Beemore** (1929) and **Ceemore** (1929) in attendance, was sold in 1939 to the Board of Trade to become the **Botwey**.

[Author's collection]

Dorothey Laird describes the destiny of the **Manchester Producer** in the history of the Paddy Henderson company:

…taken over by the Government from the scrappers and put under Henderson's management for use as a grain storage hulk. When war broke out she was commissioned as a cross-Channel munitions ship, and used in that service until the Fall of France. She was then put on the North Atlantic run, under the command of Captain Ebenezer Gordon who, at the age of 65, had volunteered to return to sea service after a considerable spell ashore. She was torpedoed while in ballast and sunk off the Northumbrian coast, but fortunately her whole crew was safely taken off.

The fortunes of the pre-war years of the 1930s are reflected in the completion of two of Manchester's present day landmarks. Defiant to the last, the city fathers ordered the construction of the Central Library in St Peter's Square at the height of the Depression. The building was completed in 1934, just as trade was beginning to pick up, and stands today as a working municipal library and archive and a symbol of the hardship of the inter-war years. But business did bounce back and Manchester was soon flourishing again. So much so that the officers of local government were soon running out of space. In truth the Town Hall, grand Victorian edifice that it is, was really unsuited to housing the numbers of office workers employed on the business of Manchester City Corporation in the late 1930s. The Town Hall extension was built on the site between the Town Hall and the new Central Library, cleverly abutting the rotunda of the latter. And in 1938 Barton Aerodrome gave up its role as Manchester's airport when Manchester Corporation opened its new airport at Ringway, south of the city.

With the upturn in trade in the second half of the 1930s, the Manchester Ship Canal Company had invested heavily in upgrading equipment. Five new steam tugs had been delivered to replace ageing and under-powered paddle tugs and in 1939 the first motor tug, the **MSC Mallard** was delivered to the 'fresh' waters of the Canal. The Manchester Education Committee booklet, *The Inland Port of Manchester, its ships and their cargoes* published in 1938 exudes:

The dock equipment is of the most modern type, and includes [about] 300 fixed and travelling cranes, 30 electric hoists, and a powerful floating crane, designed for handling lock gates up to 250 tons, general traffic up to 120 tons, and salvage work up to 250 tons. There is a hydraulic coaling crane capable of manipulating 12 ton wagons, and five floating pontoons, used mainly for discharging timber. A special feature is the remote control gear used in connection with the electric cranes. This control enables cranes to be operated electrically from the ship's deck, thus saving labour and time and greatly reducing the possibility of accident. Cargo is discharged both directly to the shore and over ship's sides into lighters and barges for transport by water…

All berths are railway connected, and the Canal Company which is also a railway company, maintains and operates over 200 miles of line, 73 locomotives and 400 wagons. Main line railways connect with the Company's system so that there is direct communication between every ship's berth and every railway station in the Kingdom. Barge traffic, although much smaller in amount, is also well provided for, as the Company owns the Bridgewater Canal, and the Port is in direct communication with all the inland waterways of the country.

The MEC booklet waxes lyrical about the port's ability to handle grain, leaving the school child, and anyone else for that matter, in no doubt about the supremacy of the port of Manchester, its liners and 'Liners:

The port has three grain elevators: two, each of 40,000 tons capacity at Manchester, and one at Ellesmere Port of 20,000 tons capacity. These are capable of performing many operations simultaneously. At No 2 Elevator, for instance, grain can be discharged from six vessels at once at the rate of 900 tons per hour. At the same time the grain is weighed, distributed to any one of 340 bins, or put into sacks, and loaded into thirty railway trucks and twenty lorries simultaneously. …floating elevators suck the bulk grain from the ship's hold, weigh it, and pass it beneath the quays on moving bands which convey it to the elevator…

Departing steamers used to set off down the Canal from Salford with almost no bunkers. They called at the Partington Coal Basin below the Irlam steel works to replenish stocks. Here, railway wagons were pulled up an incline at the top of which the coal was tipped out into chutes. These led directly into the ship's bunkers. But what a mess - there was coal dust all over the ship, floating on the canal and covering the bank as far as the eye could see. But again in charge of the tugs, fore and aft, the ship was ready to sail the North Atlantic once again.

On returning to Eastham, ships' crews could amuse themselves by guessing which vessels were visiting Manchester from inspecting the collection of funnel tops on the quayside. When coal was burned in natural draught Scotch boilers, a tall funnel was needed that had greater air draught, especially when the ship was in ballast, than the clearance of the fixed bridges along the Canal. The tops of the funnel were demounted at Eastham to give the necessary clearance and to be picked up on return. In photographs of ships of that vintage, the connecting flange between the upper and lower funnel portions can be seen, usually a little below the black top. The practice continued into the 1970s.

The funnel game: visitors from United States Lines and Strick Line were amongst those requiring surgery before proceeding above Eastham. Strick's *Karaghistan* (1957) has had much of her funnel removed and stowed on the foredeck for a paint job while at Manchester.

[Author]

On the eve of war the Manchester Liners' fleet stood at ten ships, all but two of which were coal burners with two further ships of the *Manchester Port* class on the stocks at the Blythswood Shipbuilding Company at Scotstoun. Manchester Liners had made a full recovery from the Depression and was braced once again for the rigours of war.

Ladies' comforts in the state rooms aboard the new *Manchester Port* class included an ornate pin dish made for ML by Dunn Bennett & Company of Burslem.

[Author's collection]

R Dawson Harling, ML Toronto Representative, set of three advertising cards for services from Toronto to Manchester via Montreal.

[Author's collection]

FROM *THE MEMOIRS OF VIRGINIA LORD* BY MARIANNE PILGRIM
A NOVEL BASED ON THE DIARIES OF VIRGINIA LORD BOSTICK (see references)

The following text is abstracted from *The Memoirs of Virginia Lord* with the kind permission of Marianne Pilgrim. It tells of a voyage by three young American friends travelling from Montreal to Manchester in the summer of 1938 aboard the new steamer **Manchester City** (Commodore Philip Linton):

We started from Montreal at 12.25 am, a little before schedule. There are 371 head of cattle, 52 crewmen, 30 cattle boys, and 9 passengers besides us. Additional cargo of ham, bacon, and fruit, mostly pears, were also set on the ship.

After dinner at about 7 pm a new pilot came aboard. The three of us watched the launch from the railing as it came alongside the ship bringing the new pilot with it. We passed under Quebec Bridge, seeing Chateau de Frontenac and Montmorency Falls which looked like folds of cloth from a distance and as high as Niagara Falls but not as broad. The cattle were all quieted down. If I wrote letters, the pilot would take them ashore at Quebec. I slept perfectly and July 22nd, Friday we woke to a fair weather day, very calm, with no sense of motion at all from the ship. The toilet paper in our cabin had humorous verses on each sheet, but I didn't always get the humour.

We played shuffleboard and sampled the breakfast of grapefruit, oatmeal porridge, bacon, toast, marmalade and coffee. Bovril was at 11; soup, roast beef, bread, tea, salad, pudding, and crackers for lunch at 1. After lunch we had lifeboat and life preserver drill. The crew helped us with them. Tea was served at 3.30 which also included biscuits - cookies with assorted fillings. Dinner consisted of some delicious hors d'oeuvres, soup, chicken, potatoes, cauliflower, peaches and cream, biscuits and cheese at 9.30. Aside from the hors d'oeuvres, the food was bland, typically British. After dinner Pricilla, Mary and I had a highly exciting game of shuffleboard until dark. It was a glorious sunset; turquoise, blue and gold flashed in the clouds. Supper included cheese or meat sandwiches and drinks. We had an apple served to us on deck.

The passengers played rummy in the lounge until 11.00. I got up at 3.45 to see the sunrise from our porthole. A ship passed in front of the sunrise and a slight fog came later. This started the ship's whistle blowing intermittently for over an hour. We entered The Strait of Belle Isle. We went through with fine visibility. We passed Belle Isle about midnight. It was very barren and bleak just like the two lighthouses; one was on a cliff and one below. I was not sorry to leave that land; the boat seemed cosy and home-like by comparison. We are setting our clocks ahead one half hour a day now.

A stowaway was found aboard tonight. He was an Indian who came out for food after five days. He will have to work passage and go to prison in England for about three weeks. They found a bankbook and a British passport on him. Then who knows if he would be able to stay in England.

Today is one of the many mid-ocean days, clear waters, but no sun until the afternoon. We played three games of shuffleboard in the morning, saw a whale sporting off to starboard, and saw the stowaway.

Wednesday, July 27 was a clear and beautiful blue water day. Captain Linton invited Pricilla, Mary and I up on the navigation bridge. We saw the chart room with the charts indicating soundings, depths, and the quality of bottom. We also had a Marconi echo meter demonstrated. An electric impulse goes to the bottom and returning sound waves register on a card indicating the number of fathoms by a little illuminated pointer. From there we went into the compass room, with its excellent views and two adjoining alleyways to the navigation bridge. Here was the compass, a floating card and black line indicating the ship's head, and a man turning the wheel. They worked in two hour shifts. Then up to the Monkey Island, as it was called, where we saw the stars, cloud and some extraordinary views. We also saw the direction finder and antennae for the radio man.

The captain also showed us his quarters: living room, bedroom and private bath. He explained the use of the barometer. Captain Linton, who is commodore of the fleet, also showed us the galley, where a steam stove has compartments for a dozen different foods cooking at once. The cattle stalls were like a fine, clear, large airy barn with a 660 head capacity. There was no motion at all below.

We went back to the captain's quarters and he showed us charts of where the wheat cargo was stored, and whom it was being shipped to. He showed us pictures of the first ship he sailed in 1884, one of the largest first steel ships, a square rigger named the **British Isles**. Back then, it took eight weeks to get from England to Quebec.

Another dead steer was put over board today at 6.30 am. He broke a leg and the captain had to shoot it. I didn't witness this execution. I saw another whale and a frightened egret on the horizon about a mile away.

Thursday the 28th was another beautiful clear and smooth day. There was some pitch to the ship but nothing objectionable. The captain invited us to his room again and gave us pictures of the ship and talked with us about England's preparedness, not for war but for peace. Millions of pounds were being spent; gas masks for everyone, and lectures being given on the use of them. He gave us true stories of rescues to read. One was the rescue of the entire crew of the SS **Volumnia** in 1929 by the **Manchester Regiment**, Captain Linton was in command.

At noon we docked in Birkenhead, across from Liverpool. The cattle were discharged and it was lots of fun to watch. All so cramped from ten days in the stalls, they stumbled and fell or slid from the nose to the end of the gangplank. Some emerged and looked about surprisingly and wanted to return. It took a long time to clear the ship of the cattle, hay and grain.

TABLE 2: The Manchester Liners fleet at the outbreak of World War II

Ship	Built	Gross tons	Master
Manchester Brigade	1918	6,021	Capt. F L Osborne
Manchester Division	1918	6,027	Capt. E E Bonnaud
Manchester Exporter[1]	1918	5,277	Capt. G S Ronald
Manchester Spinner[2]	1917	4,767	Capt. F Clough
Manchester Regiment	1922	7,930	Capt. E W Raper
Manchester Commerce	1925	5,328	Capt. J E Riley
Manchester Citizen	1925	5,328	Capt. G M Mitchell
Manchester Port	1935	7,291	Capt. F D Struss
Manchester City	1937	7,296	Capt. J Barclay
Manchester Progress	1938	7, 346	Capt. P Linton
Blythswood Yard No 58		7,264	
Blythswood Yard No 59		7,363	

[1] Ex **Rexmore** 1928

[2] Ex **Grampian Range** 1921

CHAPTER 6

CONVOYS, COLLISIONS AND U-BOATS

Although merchant ships were more efficient and had become larger and faster than they were in World War I, the ships were equally if not more vulnerable. Weapons were more deadly than ever despite the limitations placed on Germany by the Treaty of Versailles. The 'legal' design of the German pocket battleship produced a cruiser-type ship with the fire power of a battleship, ideal for picking off merchant shipping. Most importantly the submarine and its torpedoes could travel farther and faster. Germany had also developed a magnetic mine, which was far more effective than the contact mines used in World War I. Air power had progressed tremendously from the ponderous Zeppelins and fragile biplanes of the Great War to long range bombers and fast and well-armed fighters. Germany was also developing its rocket-propelled bombs to drop on British industry and British cities.

The pocket battleships, **Admiral Graf Spee** and **Deutschland**, along with their supply ships, had been sent into the Atlantic during August 1939 in readiness for hostilities. By 3 September 1939, 57 active U-Boats were already on station in the North Sea and Atlantic. Just nine hours after war was declared, U30 sank the Donaldson Line's **Athenia** by torpedo and then brought down the mainmast with a shell, possibly aiming for the radio aerial. Although there were 1,306 survivors out of the 315 crew and 1,103 passengers aboard, the tragedy was a clear warning to the Admiralty that the Germans were not going to abide by the rules of engagement which they had earlier been made to sign.

Immediate provision for convoys was put in place. North Atlantic convoy identification numbers were initially prefixed by ON, ONF and ONS outbound to Halifax and destinations beyond, whereas eastbound convoys were prefixed by the letters SC. In the early days the Atlantic convoys could be escorted only up to 200 miles west of Londonderry, beyond which vessels were alone and vulnerable. The convoys were organised in columns and each ship had a convoy number, for example, 47 would be stationed seventh in line in the fourth column. The columns were spaced 1,000 yards apart and each ship kept station 400 yards behind the vessel in front. The speed of the convoy was set at the speed of the slowest ship.

At night the ships were blacked out and convoy manoeuvres had to be precise and accurate to avoid collision. The lessons of maintaining exact station, of convoy course changes and of single ships acting under orders independently from the rest of the convoy were yet to be learned. On the night of 4 December the **Manchester Regiment** was steaming westwards in convoy destined for St John, New Brunswick, having earlier loaded general cargo at Manchester. At a position south west of Cape Race, Harrison Line's **Chancellor** and the Athel tanker **Athelchief** collided in the dark, the convoy trying to conceal all lights, as even the smallest glimmer could give the position of the convoy away to the enemy. The **Chancellor** was badly holed and sinking rapidly, while the tanker with her numerous cargo bulkheads remained buoyant. The **Manchester Regiment** was stationed some distance from the collision but aware of it from the signals emanating from the Commodore's vessel. One of the signals was to instruct the Pacific Steam Navigation Company's passenger liner **Oropesa** to return to the **Chancellor** to pick up survivors from the lifeboats, life rafts and the sea.

The choice of the **Oropesa** effecting rescue was twofold: she had the speed to catch the convoy up, and was fitted out as troop transport with berths for the survivors and with medical facilities. In peace time she carried 632 passengers as an intermediate cargo passenger liner. However, the downside was that she was a big ship and not an easy ship to manoeuvre at convoy speed, especially in a blacked out convoy on a dark Atlantic night. Having picked up the Harrison Line survivors the **Oropesa** was able to rev up her turbines and hasten back to the safety of the convoy. In doing so she collided in the dark with the **Manchester Regiment** which immediately started taking on water. As the one-time company flagship, the **Manchester Regiment** was hastily abandoned and quietly sank. It was then realised that nine of the ship's company had gone with her, a tragic and unnecessary loss. Little over a year later the **Oropesa** was sunk by a torpedo in the Atlantic, but this time 113 lives were lost.

An early requirement by the Ministry of War Transport was that the three existing **Manchester Port** class ships had their load line slightly increased to enable them to load increased cargo deadweight, especially deck cargoes such as military vehicles and aviation fuel in drums. To achieve this alteration, the wooden hatch boards in the tonnage opening had to be replaced by welded steel plates. As they had been designed as open shelter deck ships, it would not have been possible to convert them to fully-closed shelter deckers as the structural design of the ships would not have permitted them being loaded to the minimum statutory freeboard.

This alteration caused the **Manchester Port** to be remeasured for tonnage with the uppermost continuous or weather deck becoming the freeboard and tonnage deck rather than the 'tween or Lower Deck. This resulted in an increase in registered depth to 35 feet and an increase in gross tonnage from 5,649 to 7,291. As this was the basic means of assessing many ships' dues and costs, it can only be assumed that the increase in cargo-carrying income more than offset the increased costs that ML would have been faced with, since it elected to retain the increased tonnage after the war. A non-financial drawback was that some ships were reported to be 'very wet' when fully loaded.

The **Manchester City** was taken up at an early stage as a naval auxiliary and converted for duties as a minelayer mother ship. Under her civilian master, Captain James Barclay, the **Manchester City** was equipped with workshops and support equipment and with mines loaded in the holds was kept on duty supplying the allied minelayers in the Atlantic and North Sea. This work ended in December 1940 when she became HMS **Manchester City** and after further conversion work she set sail for the Indian Ocean. With access to Admiralty colliers carrying pulverised coal for the fast fleet escorts, HMS **Manchester City** was able to sail into a totally new arena knowing that her automatic stokers would not be her undoing.

Early in 1940 the Government commenced Operation Fish. With invasion of the UK by Germany an increasing likelihood, it was desirable to get all the gold reserves and negotiable documents in Britain away to safe keeping. These included not only British reserves but reserves sent to Britain by some of the overrun countries on the Continent. Canada was the obvious safe haven, the more so as reserves could be spent in Canada and the United States to purchase much-needed supplies. The total value of the gold that was sent across the Atlantic in 1940 amounted to £828 million of which some £25 million was dispatched per Manchester Liners. It begs the question whether the masters actually knew the value of the bullion they each had sitting in the strong-room on these voyages. David Burrell reports in his history of Furness Withy:

*Manchester Liners was responsible for shipping £25 million in eight ships: **Manchester Merchant**, **Manchester Brigade** and **Manchester Progress** each carried two consignments, **Manchester Merchant** and **Manchester Brigade** totalling £4.5 million each and **Manchester Progress** £5 million. The others carried single shipments, **Manchester Commerce** valued at £3 million and for **Manchester Exporter**, **Manchester Division**, **Manchester Port** and **Manchester Citizen** £2 million each.*

Manchester Liners' ships were all well equipped, each with passenger accommodation and all renowned for their excellent galley service. As a consequence they were preferred ships as Convoy Commodore vessels, providing comfortable accommodation for the Commodore and his staff. On 26 September 1940 the **Manchester Brigade**, sailing once again as Convoy Commodore vessel, was off Malin Head in charge of convoy OB218 bound for Halifax when she was sunk by a torpedo fired by U137. The **Manchester Brigade** had loaded at Manchester and was bound for Montreal. The speed of the sinking is reflected in the loss of 58 of the 62 men aboard, a devastating catastrophe for Manchester Liners, with friends and former crew mates lost that day, many of whom were former shipmates of the surviving crews across the entire fleet. Both the Convoy Commodore, Vice Admiral Smith, and the master, Captain Clough, were among the dead.

The first of two peace time orders outstanding from before the war at the Blythswood yard at Scotstoun was the **Manchester Merchant**. Another coal burner with automatic stokers, she was delivered in May and put under the charge of fleet Commodore Captain Frederick Struss. The **Manchester Merchant** was a quasi sister to the **Manchester City** and **Manchester Progress**, delivered before the war, save that the new ship was slightly broader in the beam and completed under austerity requirements without any of the refinements of the earlier ships. Adorned in grey and sky blue camouflage from top to toe, the

Manchester Merchant came round to Manchester to join the Canadian service. The other outstanding order was delivered almost exactly a year later as the **Manchester Trader**. Similar again to the earlier ships, she was put in the charge of Captain E W Raper and quickly became popular as a Convoy Commodore vessel on the North Atlantic. Oddly, the **Manchester Merchant** was measured with the tonnage deck at Main Deck (uppermost continuous deck) level whereas the **Manchester Trader** initially had the smaller tonnage with her depth measured just to the 'Tween Deck. However, the **Manchester Trader** was soon remeasured to bring her gross tonnage up to that of her sisters in order to allow the carriage of deck cargo.

The **Manchester Brigade** (1918) in peace time lying at the head of No. 9 dock discharging grain to the No. 2 grain elevator.

[Author's collection]

The **Manchester Merchant** (1940) sailing into the darkness of war - she was torpedoed and sunk in February 1943.

[oil painting by the author]

The **Manchester Trader** (1941) seen in civilian colours after the war complete with mini radar mast.

[Author's collection]

The Company's ships were involved in a number of exploits during 1941 and 1942 as R B Stoker recounts in his book *Sixty Years on the Western Ocean*:

*The **Manchester Progress** (Captain James Barclay) returned independent of convoy in December 1941 from Rangoon, being one of the last ships to leave this port, and fortunately escaped damage from patrolling Japanese 'planes. After a further voyage with supplies for the Eighth Army in the Middle East she returned to the Battle of the Atlantic and, in 1942, towed the motor ship **Forest**, then a 'lame duck', several hundred miles towards the safety of Iceland without a naval escort and under very difficult conditions.*

*The **Manchester Port** made a trip under Captain E E Bonnaud to the Middle East with supplies in 1941. In November 1942, equipped as a troopship with landing craft aboard she landed the first troops and stores on Apple Beach near Algiers. She followed up with a second voyage.*

*In 1941 the **Manchester Citizen** (Captain T Makin) took supplies for the Eighth Army and in 1942, under captain F L Osborne was one of the first ships to enter Bone on the North African coast and was under fire almost continuously for sixteen days and nights.*

*The **Manchester Trader**... took her part in the Atlantic, except for one voyage to North Africa in December 1942...*

*The **Manchester Spinner** was mainly on the Western Ocean, but in 1942 sailed on a nine-month voyage with supplies to India under Captain F Downing.*

In fact, the invasion of North Africa in November 1942, Operation Torch, not only involved the landing ship **Manchester Port**, along with the **Manchester Progress**, **Manchester Citizen** and **Manchester Trader**, but the **Manchester Commerce** and **Manchester Merchant** were also there. The **Manchester Commerce**, under Captain C A Walker, made two trips to North Africa. As Commodore ship on returning home, off Gibraltar, she was attacked by aircraft and her gunners were responsible for bringing down three enemy planes.

The **Manchester Division**, under Captain H Hancock, was on passage for Cape Town, when on 30 November 1942 she was instructed to stand off the Blue Star Line's **Dunedin Star** which was stranded on the 'Skeleton Coast' of South West Africa. The **Dunedin Star** had managed to get 43 crew members and 21 passengers ashore onto what was a remote, desolate and uninviting desert. They were eventually rescued overland. The **Manchester Division** was able to rescue 40 personnel off the wreck and take them to the comforts of Cape Town, while other members of the ship's company and the remaining 116 passengers were taken aboard other ships that had been diverted to the scene. A tug sent up from Cape Town was wrecked further south along the coast on its return for bunkers. The whole episode was advertised to the enemy as it relied on regular radio contact between ships, the wreck and the shore. The **Dunedin Star** was the victim of an uncharted obstruction.

Equally, it was not the enemy that almost caused the loss of the **Manchester Exporter** in December 1942. In collision in Belfast Lough, the ship was beached before she could become waterlogged and later patched up and repaired.

By 1943 the convoys had become quieter and the ferocity of the previous two years of U-Boat attacks was greatly reduced. The almost new turbine steamer **Manchester Merchant** joined convoy ON166 off the Scottish coast bound for Halifax having previously loaded at Manchester. On 21 February the convoy was systematically attacked by a pack of U-boats. The fourteenth ship to be sunk was the **Empire Trader**, managed by Shaw Savill and Albion and previously their **Tainui**. The convoy rescue ship **Stockport**, formerly a London & North Eastern Railway ferry on the North Sea, left the convoy to pick up survivors. Having dropped behind the convoy and heading towards the stricken **Empire Trader** with 91 rescued seamen and officers from various ships aboard, the **Stockport** was herself torpedoed. All hands went down with the rescue ship in the darkness. The **Empire Trader** remained afloat at this stage and an escort, HMCS **Dauphin** (K157), was detailed to accompany her to the Azores. The merchantman slowly got lower on her marks and it became apparent that she would never make port. Orders were given to transfer the crew to the escort and to scuttle the **Empire Trader**.

Convoy ON166 was quiet until daylight when the attacks started again. Two ships were sunk that day before the convoy was left in peace for the surviving ships to make port at Halifax as best they could. The last ship to be attacked was the **Manchester Merchant**, under Manchester Liners' Commodore Captain Frederick D Struss, and clearly quite a prize for any U-boat captain to report destroyed. The **Manchester Merchant** had stayed on the North Atlantic run since her delivery from the builders in 1940, save for her previous voyage when she took munitions and stores down to Algiers.

U628 fired two torpedoes into the **Manchester Merchant** causing devastation. The ship rapidly started to take on water and the order was given to abandon her. Many men were lost in the incident although others got away into the boats and rafts with some men also in the water. The wait must have been very tense, knowing that there was no longer a Convoy Rescue Ship to come for them, and knowing that many men were already missing. But the survivors were soon picked up by an escort (HMS **Montgomery**) and carried on their way towards Halifax with the vision of a billet in the Halifax Hotel on arrival. Captain Struss was rescued unconscious from the water and taken aboard a corvette (HMS **Rosthern**).

Such was the esteem held for the **Manchester Port**-class of ship that the loss of the **Manchester Merchant** was seen as justification for issuing Manchester Liners an Admiralty building licence to replace her. The keel was laid within weeks of the order being placed and construction proceeded apace. A number of changes were made in the basic design to adhere to the wartime requirement of utility rather than functionality, style and longevity. The new hull was ten feet longer than that of her predecessors but the main difference was that the new steamer was to be oil-fired rather than coal.

Two Manchester ships were lost in July 1943. On 9 July the **Manchester Citizen** was alone in ballast having sailed in unfamiliar territory from Freetown in Sierra Leone on passage to Lagos. She was spotted by U508 and torpedoed with the loss of 15 lives. The other former Manchester ship was the big meat carrier **El Argentino**, now wholly owned by Furness Withy & Company, but previously half owned by ML. The **El Argentino** was on a voyage from Glasgow to Montevideo and was part of convoy OS52. The convoy was found off Lisbon by a German bomber that quickly got the **El Argentino** in her sights and rapidly destroyed the fabric of the ship causing her slowly to sink. Four crew members died in the onslaught, but fortunately the officers were able to get the boats away and the remaining 82 crew and the six passengers were all saved.

Manchester Liners continued to voyage to the Mediterranean. The **Manchester Exporter** made several runs to Syracuse in support of the Sicilian campaign and later also voyaged to Naples. The

Manchester Commerce visited Alexandria then returned to the UK before setting off to the Mediterranean once more and then to New York - all under the command of Captain W H Downing. Having picked up a set of the old and obsolete cattle stalls en route, she loaded a shipment of mules and their drovers at New York, then shuttled between India and South Africa collecting more mules.

The ***Manchester Port*** (1935) at peace outbound above Barton in June 1962.

[Author]

But the highlight of 1943 was the delivery of the new ship from Blythswood. In October the all grey-painted ***Manchester Shipper*** nosed up the Ship Canal under the command of Commodore Struss OBE (he had received his honours in the light of the sinking of the ***Manchester Merchant***). The new oil burner, with the same configuration of single reduction gearing to a single shaft, was a hugely successful ship despite her austerity build. The open decks on the central superstructure were not plated in at the bridge front to save steel (draughty on deck though), and the bridge windows were essentially portholes with one large central window. But the greatest novelty was that she had a passenger certificate for 75. Berths for military personnel were in great demand and the 75 temporary bunks were built into a set of compartments on the Shelter Deck. The accommodation, although intended always as a temporary feature, was reputedly of good quality for a war-built ship. Crew's quarters were a bit cramped as she carried a crew of 76 including the ship's doctor. But on the plus side, extra-large messing facilities were provided. Apart from one trip to North Africa the new ship was deployed on North Atlantic convoy work.

The ***Manchester Shipper*** (1943), as built, with small bridge windows and open forward Boat Deck.

[Author's collection]

During 1943 Manchester Liners' Montreal office was charged with the management of three of the Canadian Park Steamship Company steamers built for charter to the British Ministry of War Transport. The Park Steamship Company of Montreal was formed in 1942 as a Crown Corporation. The objective of the new company was to assist the movement of supplies to the various Allied battlefronts. A total of 176 ships, to a variety of designs and representing an investment of Canadian $270 million were built in Canada for the company between 1942 and 1945. In September 1943 Captain M E Bewley took the newly-completed **Westmount Park** from her builders in Montreal; in September Captain F L Osborne took the **Riverdale Park** from the Davie yard at Lauzon, midway between Montreal and Quebec; and, in December Captain E W Espley collected the **Belwoods Park** from her builders at Sorel opposite Quebec.

The three standard wartime 'Park' ships managed by Manchester Liners were driven by triple expansion engines fired by oil. Utilitarian in the extreme, they were based on a design prepared by J L Thompson & Sons, of Sunderland. But despite their apparent fragility and despite their discomfort compared to the relative luxury of even the older Manchester Liners' vessels, they were invaluable to the war effort and Manchester Liners was proud to be in a position to offer management and crewing of the vessels. Seven other Parks were put under the management of Furness Withy & Company.

With the war slowly turning in favour of the Allies, many companies started to look to the future and peace. The new civil airport at Ringway was going to bring international trade to the area by air and ML decided it would need a slice of this post-war aviation action and duly registered as a potential company for air transport. Sadly, in 1944, Manchester Liner's Chairman, Lord Essendon died. His successor was Sir Ernest Murrant, who had earlier returned from the Middle East where he had been the representative for the Ministry of War Transport.

In the autumn of 1944 an order for a repeat of the **Manchester Shipper** was placed with the Blythswood yard for delivery as soon as possible. The order was placed with an eye to greatly improved trading conditions postwar. But by the year end the emphasis had begun to change from building anew to repairing - the tide had turned in favour of the Allies and fewer ships were being lost. Work on the new hull slowed to a snail's pace and while parts that had been ordered arrived at the yard, many were put into store or used for repair work. Work on the new build had all but stopped during the last few months of the war and her intended 1945 delivery was set to one side by both parties to the construction contract. Peace was clearly approaching and Manchester Liners, like so many others, was posturing to pick up the pieces and start again in the cold grey dawn of postwar hope.

During the course of the war, Manchester Liner's masters were repeatedly trusted with the role of Commodore for Canadian coastal convoys. In September 1945 the Canadian Naval Mission Overseas in London wrote to ML:

During the war against Germany it was frequently found necessary to detail masters of merchant ships to act as commodores of coastal convoys in Canadian waters. I have been requested by the Chief of the Naval Staff to express to you the high appreciation of the Naval Staff for the services which have been performed in this respect by the captains of your company. Particular reference is made to the following masters, who acted as commodores in the number of convoys indicated –

Captain J Barclay of East Didsbury, 6 convoys
Captain E E Bonnaud of Whaley Bridge, 13 convoys
Captain E W Raper of Old Trafford, 17 convoys, and
Captain F D Struss of Ashton-on-Mersey, 13 convoys.

Captain James Barclay was, by all accounts, quite a character. On one occasion aboard the **Manchester Progress**, he had broken convoy and sailed independently, the convoy being very slow. On arrival in Manchester he was summoned to a Naval Board of Enquiry at Liverpool, at which he offered "Gentlemen, my ship is in Manchester being discharged and I stand before you with a dry arse!" He was one of the few who could get away with such a comment.

Manchester Liners did survive the war - yes, it had lost ships and, yes, it had lost many of its men to the war, but it had survived and would rebuild its fleet and services into a vibrant member of various North Atlantic Conferences. But Manchester and many of its people had not done so well during the five years of conflict. The Luftwaffe never quite managed to bomb any of the lock gates and associated weirs on the Canal and stop the port from operating, and invariably missed the strategic factories in Trafford Park that were so critical to the war effort. But the German bombers and rockets did manage to change completely the face of the city and large swathes of its suburbs.

The devastation was immense, yet there had been some miraculous survivals. As the city pulled back the blackout material from its windows it looked out on block after block of rubble where once fine nineteenth century and younger office and factory accommodation had once stood. The Cathedral and the Chetham's Hospital School buildings, surrounded on three sides by city railway termini, the nearby Shambles, the buildings around Albert Square and St Peter's Square, these were all damaged but intact. Piccadilly was not so lucky, with much destruction and rubble heaped up on sites of dereliction that were now unrecognisable. The pre-war, perhaps rather cramped, Victorian city centre would never be the same. Cruelly, in later years, it was said that Hitler had done the city a favour by opening the door for redevelopment. But at what price and who was going to pay for the rebuilding of the city, certainly the open bomb sites later boosted profits for the National Car Parks company well into the 1960s.

Strange tales were told of the bomb that had fallen through the roof of a semi-detached house in Withington, causing damage as it fell through to the front room, and taxing the duty bomb disposal officer and his team for many an hour. There were the buckled tramlines that had isolated sections of track from the rest of the system but which would soon be replaced by rubber-tyred trolley buses, the like of which were first introduced on the run out to Ashton in 1938. There were the stories reporting the vegetable production from organised allotments in the municipal parks. And there were stories of great hardship, of heroism and gallantry from all walks of life. But above all were the personal losses that every man woman and child had borne, mothers and fathers, sons and daughters, none of whom would come home from the war; few talked of the gallantry or of the losses, though all remembered.

So if you have seen a semi in Withington with a red tiled roof and a round patch in the front of the tiles made up in non-matching pink you now know what the patch was for. If you look very closely you will also see that the brickwork is badly cracked above the downstairs windows too! More remarkable was that the Ship Canal remained intact during the Blitzkreig and that Mr Hitler never managed a direct hit on one of the many critical features retaining the water in the Canal system. The docks were bombed on a number of occasions in the 1940s, but the infrastructure was never critically damaged and was quickly repaired to maintain a vital and over-stretched port throughout the hostilities.

Manchester Liners acted as agents for many of the wartime visitors, stretching the resources of its staff to the limit. It is these same staff, shore and sea-based, that were now charged with putting the business of the 'Liners back onto a commercial peace time course.

The **Manchester Progress** (1938) in wartime grey.

[National Maritime Museum]

HOW DID THE BIG SHIPS PASS EACH OTHER IN THE SHIP CANAL?
BY HARRY HIGNETT - FORMER MANCHESTER PILOT

In the canal, ships from about 48 ft beam normally use the services of tugs, one each end. The forward tug uses two tow ropes. About 15 ft from the tug the ropes are bound together, forming a bridle. The stern tug also uses two ropes but they are used crossed, ie the port rope from the tug is made fast to the starboard side of the ship and the starboard rope to the port side. This allows the tug to pull astern and or to either side. By slowing the ship down the water passing over the rudder is more effective when maintaining the same engine speed.

The practice is to maintain the stern of the vessel in the available centre of the waterway so the propeller is least endangered. If the stern gets too near the bank it tends to cling to that side but with the bows nearer the centre of the channel the vessel will run for the other side and may become unmanageable.

When approaching another vessel it is usually at a mutually selected stretch of canal. They maintain the centre of the waterway until about half a ship's length apart. The stern tug is set to pull astern thus assisting the steerage capabilities of the ship. They each then steer towards the centre of the water between the approaching ship and the canal bank. As soon as the two head tugs are passing each other they prepare to pull their particular ship away from the bank. But when the vessels are passing each other the tendency is for each ship to dive into the wake of the other. Also the stern of the vessel is quite near one canal bank and the ship will try to run for the opposite bank. The tug is in the position to counteract the run and assist the ship into the correct position in the centre of the waterway.

The helmsman uses the rudder to steer the ship into the correct attitude for passing and, if there is any difficulty, advises the pilot who is in position to use corrective procedures.

The limited width of the Manchester Ship Canal is evident in this view of the **Manchester Courage** (1969) approaching Warburton Bridge.

[Author]

CHAPTER 7

A NEW AND GREY BEGINNING

Although Germany had surrendered in May 1945, war was still raging in the Far East. In June the Potsdam Conference issued the Allied ultimatum to Japan and in August the atomic bombs fell, one on Nagasaki and one on Hiroshima – the world was shocked into peace. Whereas World War I was followed by a short boom driven by inflation during the war years, World War II was followed by sustained business development for the next thirteen or fourteen years. But at home commodities and other materials were scarce and food, especially meat and, of course, sweets, as well as clothing remained on ration. It was a grey and austere world that beckoned after the hubbub of the victory street parties had died down. Men came home to Civvy Street wearing their ill-fitting demob suits and then had to look for work. But there was plenty to do, not only cleaning up damaged and destroyed bomb sites but also putting industry and trade back on the rails.

Mr Churchill's coalition government was voted out of office and Labour found itself in power with a significant majority under Prime Minister Clement Attlee. But a great deal of effort was needed to get the country back into peacetime working order and Attlee set about reformation with vengeance.

Manchester Liners had been able to maintain an ad hoc Canadian service from Manchester throughout the war years. The main difference to peacetime was that all imports were to the order of Government and exports had been few. Sailings were dictated by availability of ship, assembled cargo and an assembled convoy. One of the first things the ship owners needed to do in peacetime was to carry out those ship repairs, large and small, that the war had prevented being carried out and ship's crews had just had to put up with. Perhaps the worst outcome was breakdown at sea, the result of five years inadequate maintenance. R B Stoker wrote:

Peace came in 1945. Manchester Liners had started the war with ten ships. Five had been lost, but three new ships had been built, so that the Company was able immediately to resume its weekly Canadian service.

The hundreds of wartime standard ships, the 'Empires', 'Forts' and 'Parks', as well as the 'Victory' and 'Liberty' ships, their charter to the Ministry of Transport eventually completed, were put up for sale. Unlike many UK shipping companies such as Canadian Pacific in the same trade as Manchester Liners, Blue Funnel and the Harrison Line, ML did not take up any options to buy. Manchester Liners was content in the knowledge it had a ship on the stocks at Scotstoun, and that its fleet was then adequate to rebuild the Canadian trade.

The wartime standard ship **Empire Regent** (1943) was built at the Furness shipbuilding yard at Haverton Hill and became the **Beaverlodge** when she was bought by Canadian Pacific in 1952 as one of seven similar ships that formed their cargo fleet. These ships were considerably larger than their ML counterparts and maintained the London and Liverpool service to Montreal, Quebec and St John (winter).

[Author's collection]

Manchester Liners did, however, look at the possibility of acquiring a couple of the AP2 type fast 15 knot oil-fired steam turbine Victory ships, but discarded the idea because they would have required considerable modification for regular use in the Manchester Ship Canal. The tall funnels and fixed lower masts of this class would require lowering to reduce air draught while the beam of 62 feet was then untried in the Canal. Besides, the loaded draft of 29 feet could mean lightening ship at Liverpool if fully loaded to the marks. Furness Withy, however, did successfully operate one of this class out of Manchester between 1947 and 1954, the **Pacific Stronghold**, which was completed as the **Tusculum Victory**. Former Liberty type ships were commonly seen in the Ship Canal, but they had a beam of only 55 feet and a loaded draught of 27 feet. Their triple expansion engines drove them at a modest 11 knots, a poor speed compared with the 13.5 knots of the **Manchester Port** class, and Liberty ships were never a contender for Manchester Liners' post-war operations.

The three 'Parks' managed through the Montreal office since 1943 were either sold or transferred out of Manchester Liners' management during 1946. The **Riverdale Park** was sold to the Triton Steamship Company of Montreal, and remained in gainful employ under a variety of names until sold for demolition in 1968. She outlived the former **Belwoods Park** by a year, the pair demonstrating that even wartime austerity ships were adequately constructed and fit for purpose. That said, the third ship, the former **Westmount Park**, was posted missing in the Atlantic in January 1957 with a cargo of coal loaded at Philadelphia and bound for Le Havre.

At her first post-war refit the **Manchester Shipper** was demoted from her role as passenger liner to cargo ship. Her emergency passenger certificate for 75 was reduced to just twelve in single and twin berthed cabins. The cabins were installed and completed over a period of refits so that her full passenger complement was only available from 1948 onwards. Her large messroom was replaced by a dining saloon and passenger smoking room and the berths on the Shelter Deck removed to allow the ship an improved deadweight. All the **Manchester Port** class ships now had a greater refrigerated cargo capacity than the older vessels (Table 3), a reflection of the termination of the live cattle trade. At the earliest opportunity the four surviving coal burners in the **Manchester Port** class were converted to oil burning.

War is a great motivator of technological advancement. Among the many wartime initiatives, the development of radar (radio direction and ranging) had progressed from frustrating and unreliable to positively valuable. Radar had been deployed in the war on selected vessels of the Royal Navy and postwar was available as a commercial option to ship owners. Manchester Liners was offered a trial set based on the Admiralty Type 268 equipment, complete with fifty or so glowing electronic valves, specifically to test its reliability and value for navigation in the often poor visibility of the St Lawrence. The set was installed in the commodore ship **Manchester Shipper**, and she takes her place in maritime history as one of the very first merchant ships ever to enjoy the benefits of radar. The radar tests were a resounding success, the **Manchester Shipper** being able to maintain headway on one occasion when all else in the St Lawrence was hove to. At about the same time, and using the same equipment, the Canadian Pacific Line's mighty **Empress of Canada**, upgraded from **Duchess of Richmond** in 1947, made the news when she came across the Mersey Bar in a thick fog successfully to berth alongside Liverpool's Princes Landing Stage.

Within eighteen months of the **Manchester Shipper** radar trials Manchester Liners had bought and installed commercial radar sets for use in all of its ships. The Company recognised both the safety implications of the new equipment as well as its commercial benefits in keeping vessels on the move. Manchester Liners also strove to install echo depth sounders in its ships as sets became commercially available.

In 1946 Manchester Liners hosted an official visit to Canada by the Lord Mayor of Manchester and his accompanying officials as part of a trade promotion delegation. Trade was nevertheless buoyant, but the Company as well as the City Fathers were keen to encourage the now longstanding link between the Port of Manchester and Canadian interests. Manchester Liners, as always, was keen to expand its network beyond the weekly service to the St Lawrence with transhipment available into the Great Lakes during summer and St John, New Brunswick and Halifax in winter. In reality 1946 was a year of consolidation in which the Company again got back on its feet and was able to put its house in order through a major refurbishment and maintenance programme.

Work on 'Yard No. 84' at the Blythswood shipyard progressed well during 1946, although materials shortages and availability of critical parts still hindered construction. The total cost of the vessel was £447,000, well over twice the cost of the pre-war built **Manchester Progress** delivered nine years earlier. However, inflation was set to rise still further into the 1950s and beyond. Yard No. 84 was ready for launching in mid-October and took to the water with the proud name of **Manchester Regiment**. To all intents and purposes a sister of the wartime built **Manchester Shipper**, the new steamer did have a number of significant improvements and modifications and was even equipped with wireless, gyro-compass and echometer. Initially registered with a depth of just 27 feet, her gross tonnage was later increased from a modest 5,825 tons when she was remeasured with the Main Deck as the tonnage deck, bringing her gross registered tonnage into line with that of her sisters at 7,638.

The **Manchester Regiment** (1947), the seventh ship in the **Manchester Port** class, was the first post-war delivery for ML.

[Author's collection]

The launch ceremony was conducted by Mrs Dorling, wife of the Colonel of the Manchester Regiment. The ship was later presented with a gunmetal plaque of the regimental badge, the fleur-de-lys and the inscription 'This is the badge of the Manchester Regiment. It is placed here by the Regiment to commemorate the naming of the ship by Mrs Dorling, wife of the Colonel of the Regiment, on 16 October 1946'. At the ceremony aboard ship at Manchester, Colonel Dorling expressed the pleasure it gave him and the Regiment to have it in the ship in recognition of the war achievements of the Merchant Navy. Captain Struss formally accepted the plaque on behalf of Manchester Liners saying that in the battles of peace he hoped the ship would prove as worthy of the high traditions of the Regiment in time of war. The plaque had pride of place outside the entrance to the passenger accommodation.

As one of the coldest and bitterest winters in memory set in, the slowest member of the fleet, the 12 knot **Manchester Exporter** dating from 1918, was sold to Far Eastern buyers. The **Manchester Exporter** slipped her moorings at Salford and sailed down the Ship Canal for the last time, the normally dirty bank-side landscape bleached clean under a blanket of hard snow. The old ship served a variety of owners and was eventually resold for demolition in Japan at the ripe old age of forty. Her sale from the Manchester Liners' fleet anticipated the arrival of the newly completed **Manchester Regiment** which was delivered in February 1947. Commodore Struss left the **Manchester Shipper** to Captain Barclay and brought the **Manchester Regiment** through her sea trials and down from the Clyde to load at Manchester. Outwardly the new ship differed from the **Manchester Shipper** in that the Boat Deck was fully plated in forward (the **Manchester Shipper** had her forward Boat Deck plated in shortly afterwards) and the forecastle of the **Manchester Progress** had solid bulwarks whereas only the forward part spirketing plate was solid on the **Manchester Shipper**. In due course the **Manchester Shipper** had her forward superstructure amended, her mean bridge windows opened out and both the **Manchester Shipper** and the new **Manchester Regiment** later had a pair of Samson posts added at the forward end of the superstructure.

The **Manchester Exporter** (1918) seen as the **Nicaragua** under the Panamanian flag.

A big increase in work for the Manchester shore staff took place in 1947 when the Furness Pacific coast service started to share loadings to the Caribbean and east coast South American ports with the Harrison Line. This meant that not only was Manchester Liners loading agents for the Pacific fleet of Furness Withy but now also assisted the regular calls of the Harrison Line ships into Manchester. Cargo booking and documentation were still carried out by Harrisons at Liverpool with the paperwork delivered to outbound Furness steamers at Eastham on departure. The Harrison Line advertisement on the front page of the *Journal of Commerce*, which for many years was adjacent to the top of the page Manchester Liners advert, invitingly offered a monthly Caribbean service loading at Manchester for '…and other islands'.

The Furness Withy owned Prince Line and its Mediterranean service from Manchester remained under the agency of Gough & Crosthwaite's at Manchester. Manchester Liners did, from time to time, look after visits from other members of the Furness family, particularly when the Johnston Warren Line needed access to the Ship Canal.

All these additional parcels of work meant additional income. At the invitation of the Anglo-America Oil Company, Manchester Liners became agents to the Esso tanker fleet in 1947 and looked after its numerous visits to the Stanlow Oil Terminal near Ellesmere Port. This diversity of activity served to strengthen the Company in post-war years and eventually led it to widen its commercial interests to encompass road haulage and engineering interests.

During the latter part of 1947 discussions were held with William Livesay, the naval architect at Scotstoun, to develop a 'Mark II' **Manchester Shipper**-type design. In the spring of 1948 agreement on the outline design of the new type of ship was agreed and a firm order was again placed with the Blythswood yard. As it happened this was the last order that the yard would enjoy from Manchester Liners and the last of the class of ship so long ago pioneered by the **Manchester Port**. Nevertheless, the huge success of the **Manchester Port**-type design is underlined by the fact that the Blythswood Shipbuilding Company completed a total of eight variations on the theme between 1935 and the delivery of Yard No 95, launched in 1950 as the **Manchester Merchant**. Changing trading conditions required the partial redesign of the class for the last ship, the **Manchester Merchant**, but thereafter a total rethink in ship design was required to suit the shifting needs of importers and exporters.

Manchester Liners celebrated its fiftieth anniversary in 1948. The year started well with Captain James Barclay bringing the **Manchester Shipper** alongside at Montreal on 19 April ahead of the pack to win the coveted Gold Headed Cane, which was traditionally awarded to the first commercial ship to reopen the port after the winter ice over. Captain Barclay had missed the honour in 1947 - by just 15 minutes – but assisted by radar the following year he was able to pick his way up the St Lawrence with greater confidence. Captain Barclay had gone to sea at the age of 14 as an apprentice aboard the square rigged sailing ship **Cambrian Princess**. The thirteen month voyage took him to South America and back - he had been witness to many changes between those early days of sail and the modern post-war era of radar assisted navigation in steamships.

ABOVE: The **Manchester Trader** (1941)

BELOW: The **Manchester Shipper** (1943).

[John Clarkson]

[Bernard McCall collection]

Both vessels had the forward end of the Boat Deck plated over in the late 1940s.

The golden anniversary of Manchester Liners was celebrated with a party at which Captain E Henderson, representing the Manchester Regiment, was invited to cut the magnificent two-tier birthday cake adorned with a model of the **Manchester Regiment**. Managing Director Kenneth Stoker presided over the celebrations with Sir Leslie Roberts, the Chairman of the Manchester Ship Canal Company. The link between the two companies had been strengthened in January when Sir Leslie's son Tony joined Manchester Liners as a management trainee following service as an officer in the Grenadier Guards.

Tony Roberts started life in the Dock Office at No 8 Dock, progressed through all the shore departments at home and in Canada and eventually rose to the position of Chairman of the Board of Manchester Liners in 1979.

The tanker ***Esso Chelsea*** (1945) approaching the Barton bridges outbound on ML business.

[Author]

Throughout 1949 and 1950 the Company operated one and sometimes two services a week out of Manchester to the Canadian sea ports, those in the St Lawrence offered only seasonally. Chilled and frozen food imports continued to be important, and bulk shipments of liquid lard and grain were key imports. Exports included machinery, processed and electrical goods as well as luxury items. The trade was developing nicely and Manchester Liners, as always, was beginning to feel that the time was soon set for expansion.

But first, in late September 1950, the last of the ***Manchester Port*** class went down the slipway at Scotstoun. The ***Manchester Merchant*** was slightly beamier than her sisters, leaving just three feet to spare in the Ship Canal locks. She was slightly faster too, with her David Rowan turbines helping to give her a speed of up to 14.5 knots. For the technically minded, she had the normal triple turbine system geared to a single shaft to produce 5,500 shaft horse power. Three single-ended oil-fired boilers generated superheated steam for the turbines at up to 225 pounds per square inch; the bunkers could hold an impressive 1,052 tons of fuel oil. The electricity generating plant comprised two 35 kW units providing 110 volt direct current to the entire ship.

Outwardly the appearance of the new ***Manchester Merchant*** was more modern, with an oval funnel and curved bridge front with the navigation lights let into a recess beneath the bridge wings. And like all her predecessors her upper pole masts could be lowered through the mast platform into the lower mast to reduce air draft for the Ship Canal fixed bridges. This fine ship came up to Manchester in January 1951 and commenced loading for St John.

The year 1950 is perhaps best remembered as the year in which the Board decided that expansion was not only desirable but was also necessary. At its meeting on 7 November the decision was taken that

Manchester Liners would develop a direct service up the St Lawrence and beyond into the Great Lakes. For this it would require specially-built vessels of a size that would allow access to the great industrial centres like Chicago and Detroit via the narrow confines of the Lachine, Welland and Soo canals. Specially-built Lakers had run between European ports and the Great Lakes since the 1930s, confined to a 14 feet draft and a beam of no more than 44 feet. These little ships were distinctive with straight snub-nosed stems and stubby sterns to maximise deadweight given the constraints imposed by the Canadian locks.

Although the term "Laker" is traditionally used to describe bulk carriers designed for service on the Great Lakes, it is also a term of endearment for the small European sea-going ships trading to the Great Lakes before the St Lawrence Seaway opened and is used thus in the context of this book.

The **Manchester Merchant** (1951) approaching the Barton bridges in April 1967.

[Author]

The main European direct Lakes operator was the Fjell Line which benefitted from European export trade that was significantly greater than that available into the Lakes from Manchester. But the decision to follow the Scandinavians into the Lakes was not based primarily on the potential cargo revenue then available but rather on developing a firm business footprint in the Great Lakes. This posturing was a response to the joint US and Canadian agreement to develop the concept of what would one day become the St Lawrence Seaway, so allowing sea-going ships with a draft of 27 feet access to the Great Lakes. Manchester Liners wanted to be a part of the greater trade that this enterprise would bring, loading full sized ships inland at Manchester and on the other side loading the same ships inland in Canada and the United States. In the meantime little ships of no more than 44 feet beam were required to develop that trade.

So by 1950 Manchester Liners was back on its feet trading its longstanding Canadian routes. It had an eight ship fleet (six **Manchester Port** class vessels, the **Manchester Division** dating from 1918 and the **Manchester Commerce** built at Haverton Hill in 1925) and was set for expansion with new and exciting prospects in hand. In the autumn Manchester Liners turned to Cammell Laird & Company at Birkenhead and asked for a quotation for a new and advanced ship that had been worked up between them as the optimum design for the Montreal and Quebec/St John and Halifax services. Just before Christmas a contract was signed for £606,000, with keel-laying planned for the New Year. In the meantime ideas were advanced also towards the planning of a pair of Lakers, also with the team at Cammell Laird, based on optimising deadweight on a 14 feet draught.

The period 1945 to 1951 had been an austere period in which Clement Attlee had enjoyed a six year reign as Prime Minister. During this period major industry had been brought back from the brink through a programme of nationalisation, creating for example, both the National Coal Board and British Railways. Social security was greatly enhanced by the Attlee Government and, of course, the National Health Service was initiated. And at the end of his six years as premier Attlee handed power to the Conservatives with Winston Churchill once again ensconced in Downing Street.

Manchester and its hinterland returned to its feet with the wheels of industry revolving at an ever increasing speed. Ration cards were still valid for some foodstuffs and for most items of clothing, but the overall recovery of industry and demand for its products, both in the home market and overseas, meant that the British worker had money in his pocket and a little disposable income to enjoy.

MANCHESTER LINERS, LTD.

MANCHESTER.

To be forwarded to :—

Name

Passenger per s.s. "MANCHESTER   "

Sailing Date   To
                                         Landing Port

Final Destination

c/o **MANCHESTER LINERS, LTD.,**

SALFORD DOCKS, MANCHESTER.

CABIN.

Contemporary baggage label.

A GOLDEN JUBILEE

The year 1948 was the fiftieth anniversary of the formation of Manchester Liners. Mr R B Stoker (junior) wrote in an article in *Sea Breezes* in May 1948:

We have seen a steamship company pioneering in an inland port; and an example of its success has helped Manchester to become one of the greatest ports in England and to transform the 'Cottonopolis' of 50 years ago into a 'city of a thousand businesses'. A new race of inland seamen has been raised who in peace and war have proved worthy of the highest traditions of any port in the Kingdom. The present fleet (in order of increasing age) consists of:

Manchester Regiment	*Commodore F D Struss*
Manchester Shipper	*Captain J Barclay*
Manchester Trader	*Captain E W Raper*
Manchester Progress	*Captain W H Downing*
Manchester City	*Captain F L Osborne*
Manchester Port	*Captain F Downing*
Manchester Commerce	*Captain H Hancock*
Manchester Division	*Captain E W Espley.*

Manchester Liners still has in its employ some members of the staff who joined the company on its formation 50 years ago and who are still rendering silent service in helping the wheels of commerce turn. Today the name of Manchester Liners stand as high as it has done and its policy of catering adequately to the needs of the importing and exporting communities of this great industrial district is fully maintained. Even in this time of uncertainty and rapidly rising costs an order for further new tonnage has been placed. So we may hope that Manchester Liners will continue to be worthy of the men who sail them, and in the words of the Directors of the Manchester Ship Canal Company 'a credit to the nation and of singular pride to the home port of Manchester'.

Captain Frederick Downing and Captain William Downing were brothers.

TABLE 3: Refrigerated cargo space (plant by R&E Hall of Dartford, circulating brine and using granulated cork or cork slab insulation)

Ship	Built	No. of chambers	Total cubic footage
Manchester Division	1918	8	15,300
Manchester Exporter, ex **Rexmore**	1918	0	0
Manchester Commerce	1925	4	13,630
Manchester Port	1935	6	20,340
Manchester City	1937	6	20,000
Manchester Progress	1938	6	19,800
Manchester Merchant	1940	6	20,700
Manchester Trader	1941	6	19,500
Manchester Shipper	1943	4	19,820

CHAPTER 8

TO THE WEST, NORTH AND SOUTH

The early 1950s saw the Company training policy consolidated with both Deck Officer and Engineer Officer apprenticeships offered by Manchester Liners in association with a range of marine and technical colleges. Officer recruitment focussed as much as it could on the training scheme. While the engineers were set to learn the intricacies of steam turbine machinery and the various ancillary gear, the deckies gazed at the stars and learned the art of navigation. Part of the Deck Officer recruitment was convincing the Board of Trade medics of fitness, both in body and mind, and even more crucially on clarity of vision. The engineers were excused these tests on the grounds that they only had to stand on a nice warm control platform and pull a few levers now and again.

The Board of Trade eyesight test comprised a box with various holes in which arrays of coloured lights would show. The candidate had only to identify the colour of the lights. One candidate recalls being told by an elderly man sitting alongside a brilliant hissing oil lamp that he would be shown either two reds, a single red or two greens. The bright oil lamp was thrust into the box behind the faded coloured glass discs, and without a second thought he correctly shouted 'Yes, that's a yellow'. 'Dammit' responded the medic 'is it red or is it green - you are wasting my time as well as yours'! By the 1960s the test had progressed to coloured dots on card each depicting a symbol or letter by a subtle colour variation. The book of cards was flicked through at great speed and woe betide any candidate who could not keep up with reporting 'a chicken', 'number 3', 'a triangle' etc., as fast as he could because his career would end there and then.

A double Manchester Liners launch took place at Cammell Laird's Birkenhead shipyard on 30 January 1952. The new design for the Montreal and St Johns service was the **Manchester Spinner**, and she preceded the much smaller 'Laker' **Manchester Pioneer** into the water by only a few minutes. The **Manchester Spinner** was a faster ship than any of her predecessors, reflecting a need for quicker and more reliable delivery times. Whereas the **Manchester Regiment**, dating from 1947, was good for 14 knots and the younger **Manchester Merchant** a tad more than that, the **Manchester Spinner** was designed with a cruising speed of 15 knots. She was an impressive ship and her dimensions were based on the perceived Ship Canal maxima of the day, being a foot beamier than the **Manchester Merchant** and 2 feet beamier than the **Manchester Regiment**. For the next decade the builder's model of the **Manchester Spinner** was proudly displayed in the window of the St Anne's Square Company offices.

The Laker **Manchester Pioneer** (1952) seen at Chicago in experimental two-tone grey livery.

[Author's collection]

But the interest on launch day was not so much on the larger ship as on the smaller counterpart, a sister to which was already nearing completion on an adjacent slipway. The *Manchester Guardian* 31 January 1952, reported the launchings:

Without any signs of flurry, Cammell Laird & Company launched two ships within 20 minutes of each other. On one slipway was the **Manchester Spinner***, a single screw cargo vessel designed for trade between the UK and Canada. Next to it was the* **Manchester Pioneer***, which is strong enough to cross the Atlantic yet is small enough to negotiate the locks between the St Lawrence River and the Great Lakes ports... Mr Kenneth Stoker, Managing Director of Manchester Liners, spoke of two natural developments. The first was the company's decision to enter the Great Lakes trade to protect the company's home port from competition and answer demands from importers and exporters for a direct service. The second was the construction in Birkenhead of steamers for a company in Manchester where there were no facilities for building.*

The second Laker was launched just six weeks later with the name **Manchester Explorer**, this time without ceremony, her sponsor being nine year old Ann Cameron Stoker, daughter of Director Robert Stoker and granddaughter of Managing Director Kenneth Stoker. Thereafter, three brand new Manchester Liners lay in the Cammell Laird fitting out basin. The two Lakers were open shelter deckers with a forecastle and bridge. There were elevated winch platforms between the hatches, two forward and two aft, with six 5 ton and two 10 ton derricks. The crew accommodation was in two berth cabins, with single berths for petty officers. Officers and engineers were accommodated in a deckhouse on the Bridge Deck with a smoke room forward and a small sick bay aft. The Captain's suite and pilot accommodation were also on the Bridge Deck. Navigation aids were modern and reflected the confined waterways that the ships were designed to navigate: gyro-compass, radar, echo sounding and wireless telegraphy.

Meanwhile the **Manchester Merchant**, under Captain Edward Raper, arrived in the St Lawrence to drop anchor upstream of a Norwegian vessel, the latter bound for Port Alfred and waiting for ice to clear at that port. Captain Raper took a report on the state of the ice and was told that the Norwegian was planning to sail to Montreal the next day while waiting conditions to clear at Port Alfred. During the night the **Manchester Merchant** raised anchor and headed up river through the ice, followed by the Norwegian six hours later when it dawned on them what had happened. Captain Raper got to the Montreal Gold Headed Cane just twenty minutes before the faster Norwegian vessel, which returned defeated down river to her anchorage.

An unusual cargo was loaded at Manchester for Montreal aboard the **Manchester Trader** in August 1952. This was an 80 ton casting brought by road from the Dominion Engineering Works in Sheffield. Smaller castings were also carried that year all bound for a new engineering works in Montreal.

The elderly **Manchester Commerce** was disposed of in anticipation of the delivery of the new **Manchester Spinner** in July. The **Manchester Commerce** enjoyed a further 15 years trading under the Pakistani flag. The last pre-**Manchester Port** class vessel then left in the fleet was the 1918-built **Manchester Division**.

The new **Manchester Pioneer** was delivered in April and loaded at Manchester for Toronto under Captain Albert Starmer of Widnes (aged 39 and the youngest master in the fleet). The **Manchester Explorer** followed a month later under Captain John McLaren from Timperley, a man who had worked his way up through the ranks and who was then in his fourteenth year with Manchester Liners. The two ships were designed to provide a monthly departure.

The **Manchester Pioneer** (1952) after lengthening, sailing from Manchester on 7 October 1962 on her last voyage before being sold.

[Author]

The inaugural sailing arrived at Toronto with the town band playing on the quay while Captain Starmer presented a ship's bell on behalf of the Manchester Chamber of Commerce to the Toronto Board of Trade, so cementing a firm link between industry in both Manchester and Toronto. On board that trip was a large prototype computer built in Manchester by Ferranti Limited for the National Research Council of Canada and ready for installation at Toronto University. As the new seasonal Lakes service settled in, the need to tranship Lakes cargoes at Montreal ceased and shipping costs were greatly reduced – indeed a whole new market was opening to the industrialists of north-west England.

The service was not all hazard free and congestion at Toronto delayed cargo handling that first season. Trimmed to no more than 14 feet the vessels negotiated 21 locks inwards with just 6 inches to spare, but on return they missed three of the shallower locks coasting down deep-water rapids. Modern-day health and safety regulations would surely no longer allow the locking in and out procedure that was adopted by the two ships; on approaching a lock the most athletic member of the deck crew was swung ashore from the 'Lakes boom', right forward, and he then had to run ahead up the lock to secure the ropes.

During August the **Manchester Explorer** completed discharge at Toronto and proceeded 'up hill' through the Welland Canal to the small town of Wallaceburg, which is near Detroit. Captain Freeman, the resident Furness Withy Superintendent logged the ship's arrival:

*At 7 pm 11 August, the vessel moored, but it took an hour to turn her round and this was done in front of the Mayor and over 100 towns people on the wharf and many more on the other side of the river and across the two bridges. The **Manchester Explorer** steamed through the narrow bridge, branches sweeping decks as she passed through with inches to spare. By the time the stern had cleared the road bridge the bow was close to the piles set in the lawn at the park, where the head rope had to be made fast to facilitate turning the vessel around. During this manoeuvre the stern came closer to the wharf and I could see that the ship had to move at least 10 feet ahead. Suddenly I was aware that the bow was underneath the trees in the park at the other side of the river. Branches snapped sharply as the vessel tried to go ahead those few feet. Captain McLaren shouted some instructions to the Chief Officer on the forecastle-head. The Chief's head appeared among the branches which enveloped the after end of the forecastle. He said 'We are all tangled up in trees here'. I apologised to the Mayor, who was standing with me, for breaking his trees. He replied ' Don't worry, they needed pruning anyway'.*

That evening the ship was alive with visitors as the watching crowd determined to inspect the foreigner with its Red Ensign proudly flying at the stern. Loading was completed early in the second morning and the **Manchester Explorer** bade her farewells to her new-found friends at lunch time on 13 August.

The new Lakes service had caught the imagination of industrialists in both England and Canada. Inland UK to inland Canada and USA spawned at least one newspaper headline. Towards the end of that first season the ships were pretty nearly fully booked down to the obligatory 14 foot draught and it was obvious that additional tonnage would be necessary for the 1953 season. To bring the Lakers down to their marks for the return Atlantic crossing, cargo was also loaded below Montreal at ports such as Chicoutimi, Rimouski, St Anne des Monts, Grande Vallée and Campbellton for discharge at Ardrossan or Preston en route for Manchester.

That winter the Company bought the six year old Norwegian Laker **Vigør** from S Ugelstads Rederi A/S and renamed her **Manchester Prospector**. She was the only member of the ML fleet ever to be equipped with combination triple expansion machinery and a low pressure turbine. She was given an extensive refit and dispatched to load at Manchester in the spring complete with traditional black hull. She soon opened another inland port to the Company, when she was the first British ship ever to berth at Leamington. The livery of the three Lakers tended to vary year by year, being traditional black with red boot topping at one stage, and even briefly grey hull and superstructure.

The **Manchester Spinner** was in service in July 1952 and carried Managing Director Kenneth Stoker as a passenger to Montreal on her maiden voyage. The **Manchester Spinner** acquired quite a reputation for herself; by November 1952, on just her fourth transatlantic trip, she took just six days to cross to Halifax. Her passenger accommodation was a delight, and included a small lounge complete with a ceramic fireplace, a mini version of the very best that any of the crack North Atlantic passenger liners could offer. A consort for the **Manchester Spinner** was soon ordered from Cammell Laird for delivery in time for the 1955 Montreal season; this was to be the **Manchester Mariner**. The elderly **Manchester Division** was later dispatched to the breaker's yard at the end of 1953.

The **Manchester Prospector** (1947) in Lake Ontario.

[oil painting by the author]

The **Manchester Prospector** (1947) in ice in the Lachine Canal.

[Manchester Liners Old Shipmates Association]

Commodore Frederick Struss DSC, OBE took the **Manchester Spinner** into Montreal behind an ice-breaker to be awarded the Gold Headed Cane at the end of March in 1954. He docked unaided as the harbour tugs were still frozen in. The wash from the two ships pulled the ice from the banks, closing the approaches to the port for a further week so that the **Manchester Spinner** was ready to depart before the next ship could attempt to navigate up to Montreal. The Commodore, whose seagoing career had started on the sailing vessels **Seafarer** and **Wayfarer** owned by W H Potter & Sons of Liverpool, retired on return to Manchester but sadly died within a year, before being able to enjoy his new-found leisure.

The **Manchester Spinner** (1952) outbound below Barton on 25 September 1966.

[Author]

The **Manchester Shipper** and **Manchester Pioneer** were involved in an unusual rescue in August 1954 when an American military plane ditched in mid-Atlantic following failure of its engines. The **Manchester Pioneer** was able to co-ordinate the rescue in which five ships formed up abreast to scour the area despite heavy weather. The two Manchester Liners took on board the four survivors although nineteen other crew members from the plane were lost.

A new service to the north was introduced in July 1954 when the chartered **Cairnavon** sailed from Manchester to Churchill, Manitoba. The port had a very short season from July only until October and just four round trips were planned, but in the event only one more trip took place that year, sailing from Manchester in August. The reasoning behind the service was that it provided an easier export route for Canadian grain from the Prairies while also allowing access to Hudson Bay for British exports. The four passenger berths that were on offer were totally oversubscribed for both return voyages. The Cairn Line, owners of the **Cairnavon**, had been in the Canadian trade from north-east England for many years and was part of the Furness Withy group.

Manchester Liners was again closer to Furness Withy than it had been for some time as the Furness shareholding had increased substantially subsequent to the 50% hike in the authorised capital of the company to £1.5 million during 1953. The Hudson Bay service was repeated the following year using the **Manchester Progress** but was not resumed thereafter as tonnage was at a premium on the main west coast routes. One officer from the **Manchester Progress** was heard to liken Churchill to the 'Wild West' describing it as 'a one horse town complete with hitching rail outside the saloon'.

The reason for the shortage of ships at this stage was the reintroduction of the tobacco and cotton run from the southern states of America. A service to New Orleans and Galveston had been abandoned before the Great War (Chapter 2) but the new route now included the ports of Charleston, Savannah and Jacksonville. This time more buoyant freight rates were forthcoming and a monthly service was commenced. The **Manchester Mariner** was launched by Mrs Clive Stoker, daughter in law to the Managing Director. The *Manchester Guardian* 29 October 1954 reported:

*Speaking after the launching at Birkenhead yesterday of the cargo steamer **Manchester Mariner**, Mr Kenneth Stoker, Managing Director of Manchester Liners, said his company would face a serious threat from the opening of the St Lawrence Seaway in the spring of 1959. At present his was the only British company operating a service to the Great Lakes although there were many foreign companies operating there.*

The delivery of the **Manchester Mariner** in March 1955 gave the Company independence from the summer charter market in order to maintain all its services. Vessels belonging to the Irish Shipping Company such as the **Irish Elm** frequently appeared in Manchester Liners' sailing lists for single and sometimes multiple transatlantic voyages. Like the Manchester Liner ships, the Irish vessels all offered twelve passenger berths. The new **Manchester Mariner**, of course, offered the normal high quality accommodation for twelve passengers in one and two berth outside cabins; some with a shower room/bath, complete with a smoking room, dining room, lounge and Promenade Deck.

Almost coincident with the delivery of the **Manchester Mariner**, Captain F Osborne of the **Manchester Spinner** received the Gold Headed Cane from the Montreal Port Authority, the second year running for the **Manchester Spinner**. The following year the **Manchester Spinner** had to concede the award of the Gold Headed Cane for opening the port of Montreal to her good colleague the **Manchester Regiment**. The inaugural sailing up to Chicago was taken by the Laker **Manchester Explorer** under Captain W E G Oliver in April 1956, an event that was keenly reported in the shipping press. Captain Oliver had joined ML as an apprentice in 1916 and his first command had been the **Manchester Division** of which he took charge in 1951.

AWARDS OF THE MONTREAL GOLD HEADED CANE TO ML

The Gold Headed Cane, originally awarded as a silk-lined Top Hat, is a long-standing tradition that dates back to the 1840s. The award was designed to promote maritime links with Europe and to encourage the early opening of the navigation season to Montreal in spring, a port that was seasonally isolated from the rest of the world by winter ice.

3 May 1926	**Manchester Regiment**	Captain J R Foale
19 April 1948	**Manchester Shipper**	Captain J Barclay
13 April 1952	**Manchester Merchant**	Captain E W Raper
30 March 1954	**Manchester Spinner**	Captain F D Struss
5 April 1955	**Manchester Spinner**	Captain F L Osborne
2 April 1956	**Manchester Regiment**	Captain F Downing
4 April 1957	**Manchester Mariner**	Captain E W Raper
1 January 1972	**Manchester Crusade**	Captain D Millard
1 January 1978	**Manchester Concorde**	Captain E Askew
2 January 1985	**Manchester Challenge**	Captain J McKay

THE HEYDAYS - POST-WAR AWARDS OF THE GOLD HEADED CANE

12 April 1946	**Fort Spokane** (1943)	Watts, Watts & Company for Ministry of War Transport
21 April 1947	**Beaverburn** (1944)	Canadian Pacific Steamships
19 April 1948	**Manchester Shipper**	
7 April 1949	**Mont Alta** (1944)	Montship Lines, Montreal
17 April 1950	**Beavercote** (1947)	Canadian Pacific Steamships
13 April 1951	**Danaholm*** (1939)	Swedish America Line
13 April 1952	**Manchester Merchant**	
2 April 1953	**Seaboard Star** (1944)	Seaboard Shipping, Vancouver
30 March 1954	**Manchester Spinner**	
5 April 1955	**Manchester Spinner**	
2 April 1956	**Manchester Regiment**	
4 April 1957	**Manchester Mariner**	

* The ice strengthened **Danaholm** was the first motor ship to win the coveted Gold Headed Cane

The **Manchester Explorer** (1952) as built with closed in forward Boat Deck.

[Author's collection]

Manchester Liners was involved in the first independent British-owned air cargo service. In 1954 Furness Withy, jointly with the Blue Star Line, purchased a large shareholding in Airwork Limited. The company was formed in 1928 and was focussed originally on personnel training. It acquired a number of Viking aircraft in the late 1940s that were used mainly as troop transports. In 1954 it commenced a transatlantic freight service with Furness Withy acting as freight agents on both sides of the Atlantic. The Airworks company's main income, however, was a lucrative transport service to the Far East.

Furness Withy wanted to appoint Manchester Liners as the Manchester agent for the Airwork freight service. Manchester Liners agreed conditional on flights being inaugurated from Ringway Airport and this was conceded. Within months the tonnages lifted from Manchester exceeded those from any other British or European airport and the new service was heralded a great success. Among the cargoes carried across the Atlantic from Manchester was Donald Campbell's record holding speedboat **Bluebird**. But to succeed in the longer term, Airwork knew it had to win a Government subsidy to carry the mail and government assistance to help it towards carrying passengers. Neither was forthcoming and the cargo services were run down, although the elderly Vikings were replaced by Viscount aircraft in the late 1950s. In 1960 Airwork was merged with Hunting-Clan to form British United Airways, a forebear of British Caledonian.

Two new Lakers joined the fleet in 1956, the **Manchester Vanguard** in April followed by sister **Manchester Venture** a month later, but not before Captain Fred Downing and the **Manchester Regiment** had taken the Montreal Gold Headed Cane. The new Lakers were really innovative little ships, as they were both the first motor ships in the fleet and the first to be ordered from an overseas builder. The pair was built at Bremerhaven in Germany by A G Weser and was equipped with 8-cylinder Deutz oil engines which provided a cruising speed of 12.5 knots. Engines and accommodation were aft. The helmsman looked from the bridge windows through two sets of hefty tripod masts for a view forward. In the Manchester Ship Canal he might have no sight at all of the forward tug save for the top of its mast should the ship be light and poorly trimmed.

Nothing could have been further from the standard single propeller turbine steamer that was then the mainstay of the fleet. The little ships were ice strengthened and fit for both the rigours of the Atlantic and the confines of the respective inland waters their trade would have them ply in both the UK and North America. In winter their design allowed them into the seasonal fruit trade on charter to Yeoward Line Ltd running up from Madeira and Las Palmas, ensuring a year round income to their owners. The relatively light design of the pair compared with the older steam turbine Lakers, combined with their blunt, flareless and straight bows suggests that they could be quite wet in heavy weather. But the shippers loved the little ships and, without doubt, the **Manchester Vanguard** and **Manchester Venture** served to consolidate Manchester Liners' foothold in the Great Lakes trade.

UPPER: The **Manchester Mariner** (1955) approaching Mode Wheel locks on 20 June 1959.

CENTRE: The **Manchester Mariner** (1955) above the Barton Swing Aqueduct on 25 September 1966.

LOWER: The **Manchester Regiment** (1947) opposite Irwell Park Wharf outbound on 7 July 1962.

[Author]

The little Laker **Manchester Vanguard** (1956). Note the 'Lakes boom' forward for landing crew members on the lock wall to assist berthing.

[Author's collection]

It was only in 1956 that Charles Hill's Bristol City Line started a rival British Great Lakes service with the ice-strengthened steamer **Toronto City**. This vessel had a poor start to life, being laid down at Boele's Scheepswerven at Bolnes in 1945 with the intended name of **Leine**, but was launched two years later unnamed. After a protracted lay up she was taken to Aalborg Værft, and was finally completed in February 1949 for J Lauritzen as the **Leena Dan**. She was an attractive ship to Hill, not only because of her Laker dimensions but also because she was equipped, like the **Manchester Prospector**, with Hill's preferred power unit, the combination triple expansion engine and low pressure turbine with double reduction gearing. Charles Hill of Bristol, keen to get into the Lakes, bought her at a premium price before getting the 'little ship' ready for her first voyage under the Red Ensign.

By 1963 the role of the **Toronto City** as a Laker had long been overtaken by the new St Lawrence Seaway and she was resold to the Greek flag. She was always a popular ship with Bristol crews, not because they enjoyed being tossed about in mid-Atlantic in a snub-nosed and stubby vessel but because they greatly enjoyed their forays into Canada. Stories are told to this day of the incredible lift in the flights of locks below Lake Superior and of the friendly welcome they always received at the smaller towns. Such was the help afforded the Lakers that at one town the fire brigade turned out to lay a quarter of a mile of hose pipe to enable the **Toronto City** to take on water.

Meanwhile, the Bristol City Line had equipped itself with five modern cargo liners, three of which, the **Birmingham City**, **Gloucester City** and **New York City**, also had combination triple expansion low pressure turbines, and was a keen and efficient competitor to ML operating out of the Severn ports.

The only other British company to operate dedicated post-St Lawrence Seaway Lakers was the Bowater Steamship Company which commissioned six identical diesel freighters of the **Elizabeth Bowater**-class between 1958 and 1960. These were used to carry paper and pulp from Bowater plants in Canada, and also in northern Europe, to its paper mills in the UK, notably on the Ship Canal at Ellesmere Port, at Dartford on the Thames and the Sittingbourne mill in Kent which was served by a quay on the Swale. Ironically one of the first ships owned by Bowaters, the **North Brook**, was very much a Laker as she was built at Duluth in 1919 as the **Chautauqua** for US Government service on the Lakes. She was acquired in 1940 when Bowater's Newfoundland Pulp & Paper Mills, the shipping arm of which was managed by Furness Withy until 1957, was concerned that the wartime charter priorities might preclude the transport of paper and pulp.

Bowater's Newfoundland Pulp & Paper Mills' Laker **North Brook** (1919) was built at Duluth originally for US Government service in the Great Lakes. We see her as **Frances**, her later name.

[Author's collection]

Montreal was again opened by Captain Edward Raper in 1957, this time aboard the **Manchester Mariner**, the fourth consecutive year that the award had gone to Manchester Liners. Captain Raper reported:

Tuesday at daybreak – April Fools Day – we decided to take a crack at it. The ice was far too thick to ram right into, so we zig-zagged along for 90 miles until finally at 1030 pm that night we broke free. We were then off Heath Point at the eastward end of Anticosti Island. We encountered a little ice near Orleans Island and reached Quebec at 4 am. We left at 0940 am after being told it was safe to proceed. There was some scattered ice en route to Montreal.

Darkness fell as we reached the East End Oil Docks, but it was not too difficult to find our way in. Chief Engineer A D Bogle had trouble with ice clogging the cooling water intakes, but otherwise the ship was able to proceed at reasonable speed.

Also in 1957 an order was placed for a new ship for the Montreal and St John service, this time from Harland & Wolff at Belfast. Launched in December 1958 as the **Manchester Miller**, she was at best a peculiar ship and the Company directors must later have questioned the wisdom of the order. Her engines were placed right aft but were the same tried and tested steam turbines of the other main line ships and connected to a single shaft. The difference was that these were more powerful engines with double reduction gearing that would provide a design speed of a very fast 17 knots. Although the speed upgrade over other fleet mates might be a selling point to some shippers, particularly the fast parcel trade, the extra fuel requirements for such speeds and the associated costs were justifiable for only a brief few years.

The **Manchester Miller** (1959) with red and black uptakes outbound at Barton on 30 October 1966.

[Author]

The **Manchester Miller** (1959) above Barton without funnel markings in June 1962.

[Author]

The **Manchester Miller** was flush decked and had an amidships bridge structure with two hatches forward and three aft. She required a crew of 50 officers and men. Like her predecessors she had twelve passenger berths in single and twin berth cabins, a saloon and small smoke room. The ship offered a massive 600,000 cubic feet hold space and was designed to the optimum dimensions of the Manchester Ship Canal. The bridge front of the vessel had a modernistic curve to it that was really the only discerning outward feature of the whole vessel, as placed right aft were twin uptakes abreast each disguised as Samson posts, which provided a distinctly unbalanced and spiky profile.

The year 1958 was the 60th anniversary of Manchester Liners and this was celebrated. Robert Stoker wrote in *Sea Breezes*, July 1958:

With fourteen ships at sea, compared with eight ten years ago, the company will face the challenge of the St Lawrence Seaway within a year. It will not be an easy trade. Competition will be severe and problems will abound.

The boilers aboard the **Manchester Shipper** were replaced in 1958. Made in Manchester and delivered to the docks, the boilers were loaded into the ship's hold and she then sailed in ballast for Cardiff and dry-docking. Here, shell plates and frames were removed to allow the exchange of boilers, new for old.

In anticipation of the opening of the new St Lawrence Seaway in 1959, Manchester Liners placed orders for a pair of fast 4,500 ton motor ships with Austin & Pickersgill at Sunderland. This pair (Chapter 9) was truly imaginative and the design of these ships was carefully matched to the anticipated freight demands and to the navigation of these larger Lakers through the St Lawrence Seaway.

But 1958 was also the year of the Munich Air Disaster. On 6 February the plane carrying the Manchester United team home from matches in Eastern Europe landed at Munich for fuel. It crashed on the third attempt to take off in deteriorating snowy conditions. Eight players were killed, survivors included manager Matt Busby and players Bobby Charlton and Jackie Blanchflower, although Blanchflower and Johnny Berry were never able to play football again. Once over the initial shock, Manchester was in mourning for several weeks. Busby was two months in hospital and a year in recovering from the crash when once again he built up a new team of 'Busby Babes', this time with names such as George Best and Denis Law.

SELLING THE PASSENGER SPACES

A colourful brochure was issued in the early 1950s to advertise the merits of a passenger berth with ML:

Over 50 years ago, Manchester Liners pioneered the transport of passengers in cargo liners. Since that time continual care and study has enabled us to maintain our lead in the art of making passengers comfortable. It is the genuine welcome, atmosphere of intimacy and the knowledge that you are an important member of the ship's company, not just a cabin number, which undoubtedly explains the very real attraction of a passage in a Manchester Liner. It is undeniable that an air of romance, of adventure, still pervades the cargo liner ... the ship that works, works hard for her living. And yet we can honestly say that the passenger accommodation on our ships is both tasteful and eminently comfortable. Cuisine is of an extremely high standard and fine chefs sail under our house flag. We believe that the combination between the thrill of seafaring aboard a merchant ship, and the restful comfort enjoyed by our passengers, explain the large number of people who will travel no other way ...

Handbill: Passage rates and sailings for the summer season of 1954. Note en suite facilities first introduced, and then only available aboard, the new ***Manchester Spinner***.

A Wedgwood plate commissioned by Manchester Liners to commemorate the 60th anniversary and the forthcoming opening of the St Lawrence Seaway. It shows the ***Manchester Pioneer*** in the Welland Ship Canal with a map of the Seaway around the perimeter.

[Author's collection]

CHAPTER 9

BOOM TIME AND THE ST LAWRENCE SEAWAY

Sailing miles from Manchester:

St John's, Newfoundland	2,030
Halifax, Nova Scotia	2,493
Quebec	2,600
St John, New Brunswick	2,710
Montreal	2,800
Churchill, Manitoba	3,070
Port Arthur, Ontario	4,029
Chicago, Illinois	4,041
Duluth, Minnesota	4,130

The year 1959 was a very special one for Manchester Liners. It was the year in which Her Majesty Queen Elizabeth II and President Dwight D Eisenhower opened the St Lawrence Seaway connecting the St Lawrence with Lake Ontario. Apart from the **Manchester Miller** arriving at Manchester to load for the first time it was also the year in which that delightful pair the **Manchester Faith** and **Manchester Fame** arrived to load for the first time – for Detroit, Chicago and Cleveland courtesy of the St Lawrence Seaway. They arrived from their builders in Sunderland freshly painted in a new livery of pale green hull, dark green boot topping and cream upperworks, all designed to keep the cargo space cool in summer sufficient for the carriage of lard in cartons.

The **Manchester Fame** (1959) outbound below Barton on 7 January 1968.

[Author]

The **Manchester Faith** and **Manchester Fame** were engines aft, bridge forward flush deckers, manned by a crew of 38 and equipped with first class accommodation for 12 passengers. They were of modest proportions - intermediate in size for the new era of the St Lawrence Seaway, neither as small as the older Lakers, such as the **Manchester Pioneer** and the **Manchester Vanguard**, nor as big as the turbine steamers running to Montreal and St John and down the eastern seaboard.

The **Manchester Faith** (1959) inbound above Barton on 8 June 1962.

[Author]

TELEPHONES:
BLAckfriars 1641 (7 LINES)
DEAnsgate 8383 (8 LINES)
DOCK OFFICE:
TRAfford Park 2721 (6 LINES)

TELEGRAPHIC AND
CABLE ADDRESS:
"NAUTICUS"
MANCHESTER.
TELEX NO. 66-220

BRANCH OFFICE:
305, India Buildings,
Liverpool, 2.
Tel. No. Central 3272.

MANCHESTER LINERS LIMITED.

ML

MANCHESTER LINERS HOUSE ÷ ST. ANN'S SQUARE,
MANCHESTER, 2.

OUR REF. CAS/HG.

N. S. Robins, Esq.,
15, Brooklawn Drive,
Withington,
Manchester, 20.

YOUR REF

11th April 1962.

Dear Sir,

    Thank you for your letter of the 9th April concerning the
"MANCHESTER MERCHANT" and the "MANCHESTER FAITH".

    You are certainly very observant and the only information
we can give is that yesterday's noon position for both vessels were :-

"MANCHESTER FAITH"	51.22 N.	09.57 W.	13.44 knots.
"MANCHESTER MERCHANT"	51.24 N.	10.24 W.	14.87 knots.

and we would think the "MERCHANT" will arrive in Montreal first.

    Yours faithfully,

C A Skelton

Letter to the author, signed by C A Skelton.

The first of the pair to be delivered was the **Manchester Faith**. She was loaded in March for the Lake ports with Captain John McLaren of Dundee in command. Anticipating the opening of the St Lawrence Seaway she sailed on the same tide as the **Manchester Miller**, both ships on their maiden voyages. The **Manchester Faith** was ninth ship in the first convoy of commercial shipping through the St Lawrence Seaway having been inspected both by ML Chairman Kenneth Stoker and the Chairman of Canadian Pacific while waiting her turn to lock in. The latter was so impressed by the vessel that he dispatched orders for similar ships to be built to enable his company to trade successfully into the Lakes as well. These were the **Beaverfir** and **Beaverpine**-type ships of the early 1960s.

Canadian Pacific's **Beaverpine** (1962) was a derivative of the **Manchester Faith** and **Manchester Fame**.

[Author]

The move into the Great Lakes with the **Manchester Faith**, which was designed to test the waters, was a bold move on the part of Manchester Liners. The economics of the smaller 14 feet draught ships was not a problem, but to fill the new larger ships for the return journey to Manchester they would need to load grain in addition to the smaller cargo parcels on offer at the Lakes ports. Besides, once the St Lawrence Seaway opened, all manner of companies would want to muscle in to the new trade and competition as prophesied by Stoker did indeed intensify. Fortunately many of the ships deployed by other companies were unsuitable and Manchester Liners at least had a head start. The key to success was the difference in freight charges between grain brought by rail to the traditional tidal ports in the lower St Lawrence and sea freight direct from ports such as Chicago. The gamble paid off and it was not long before the **Manchester Faith** was bringing bulk grain into Manchester along with bulk lard carried in special tanks. That first year she was supported on the service as before by the five smaller Lakers, also smart in the new green livery, and these vessels added Duluth to their schedule to test if the grain grown in the Prairie States could indeed be shipped directly from the head of the Lakes. The **Manchester Fame** was delivered that winter ready to take up the lakes trade in the spring.

On the main line services, ownership of the grotesque **Manchester Miller** was perhaps fortunately concealed by her anonimity - but this was not to last long. The Directors, who chose not to give the ship a proper funnel and a proper identity, chose instead to follow the lead of the American Lykes Bros. Steamship Company and Japanese Mitsui Sempaku KK and paint the name of the company in vulgar letters along the ship's hull. Text on the hull was first applied to the Lakers, which in the 1959 season came up the St Lawrence in their green livery defaced by the wording MANCHESTER LINERS LTD in black. It was an unfortunate practice that led eventually to the modern day logos and text that adorn so many ferries, virtually all the container carriers and even the commonplace coaster. The black-hulled steamers not presently destined for the Lakes also had the wording applied in white, the **Manchester Miller** among them. The wording was shortened to MANCHESTER LINERS in later years.

The Duluth service was so successful that the larger turbine steamers were put on the run. The **Manchester Progress** was first to arrive and she loaded grain and edible oils. This development allowed the oldest of the small lakers, the **Manchester Prospector**, to be chartered out for timber carrying, later to be disposed of. She traded under the Greek flag for a further decade and a half. Work for the **Manchester Explorer** and **Manchester Pioneer** was not forthcoming in the winter of 1959/1960 and the pair was laid up. Towards the end of the winter season the **Manchester Pioneer** was taken in hand by Manchester Dry Docks and a new 40 foot section inserted to provide additional hold space forward of the old No.2 hatch. The work was found not to be cost effective as the enlarged deadweight was still inadequate to satisfy the growing freight demand in the Great Lakes and plans to lengthen the **Manchester Explorer** as well were dropped.

At the 62nd Annual General Meeting Kenneth Stoker reported a disappointing year hampered by strikes:

At our General Meeting last year I felt it my duty to warn shareholders that if freight rates did not improve and costs continued to rise then, in combination, they were bound to have an adverse affect on dividend levels; unfortunately this has proved to be the case. Not only has intense competition for certain classes of homeward traffic kept freight rates in those commodities at a low level but increasing costs of labour and the prolongation of strikes in the US and in this country have contributed largely to the year's disappointing results.

Amusingly, in an article in the *Manchester Guardian*, 4 June 1959, Kenneth Stoker described how he and his brother were introduced into the 'family firm' during the school holidays at the age of 12:

I don't know that we opted for it particularly, but the Governor thought it would be good for us. We were stuck in different departments, where we entered things in books and out of books onto bills of lading. It had a certain value…

Work for the **Manchester Explorer** was found when a heavy derrick was added for charter to the Chimo Shipping Company (managed by Crosbie & Company, St John's, Newfoundland) trading seasonally from Montreal on coastal duties northwards to places such as Port Chimo, Baffin Island, north Hudson's Bay and Goose Bay. At each port of call cargo was lifted over the side into barges and taken ashore. The **Manchester Explorer** was sold to Chimo Shipping two years later adopting the more appropriate name **CA Crosbie** and later changing to **PM Crosbie**.

As trade developed from the Great Lakes so the smaller Lakers were withdrawn. The little **Manchester Vanguard** and **Manchester Venture** were initially employed on charter work for the fruit runs up from the Canaries and Mediterranean. In 1961 the **Manchester Venture** was bought by the General Steam Navigation Company of London to service its Portuguese and western Mediterranean routes to be followed also by the **Manchester Vanguard** in 1963. The ships were given traditional GSN bird names, respectively **Philomel** and **Sheldrake**, until sold on to Israeli owners in 1968.

To cope with the need to put the larger turbine steamers on Lake runs in summer a number of seasonal charters were arranged. The first of these was within the Furness Withy group when the **Western Prince** and **Southern Prince** transferred their allegiance to Manchester Liners in 1960. While the **Western Prince** remained on charter, the **Southern Prince** returned to Prince Line duties in the winter to maintain its round-the-world service. Irish Shipping also provided seasonal tonnage with any one of the motor ships **Irish Alder**, **Irish Larch** or **Irish Maple** flying the Manchester Liners house flag. A variety of other vessels were chartered in the early 1960s but the need for new dedicated tonnage to service the burgeoning market in the Great Lakes was inescapable.

There were, however, a couple of setbacks. An unofficial seamen's strike lasting six weeks took place in the summer 1960. Although this did produce some nail biting, the Liners were able to sail largely because of the Company's excellent reputation for on board creature comforts – television and good food. In one case, the picket line was recruited off the quayside to allow a sailing with a full crew complement! The second setback occurred the following spring when Cooper's fully laden but rather elderly sand barge the **Mary P Cooper** sank following a collision in the Ship Canal at Warrington. The Canal was closed for four weeks, requiring the diversion of inbound ships and a delay in sailing of three and a half weeks for the outbound **Manchester Progress**.

Prince Line's handsome **Southern Prince** (1956) spent several seasons under the ML house flag but retaining Prince Line name and colours.

[John Clarkson]

ML had to rebut the apparent poor behaviour of its officers and men when Shelagh Delaney's play *A Taste of Honey* was released as a film in 1961. It was shot partly aboard the **Manchester Pioneer**, during a winter off-season charter, to work on the Ship Canal, and partly aboard the **Manchester Shipper** on a regular liner voyage down the Canal. The sailor, a heavy drinker who is key to the whole story, abandons his pregnant girlfriend and steps nonchalantly from the Bridgewater Canal overbridge at Barton directly on to his ship ready for departure to Canada - a 15 foot leap in reality! Once on board, our man is met by an equally drunk Chief Officer! ML later cheered up and conceded that any publicity has to be good publicity!

In 1961 discussion took place with Smith's Dock Company on the Tees regarding the design of large engines-aft motor ships with their own cargo handling gear to develop the Great Lakes trade. The outcome was the **Manchester Commerce**, **Manchester City** and **Manchester Renown**. The **Manchester Renown** was registered under the ownership of Beaver Industries, owned in turn by Smith's Dock, and delivered under bareboat charter to Manchester Liners. Powered by a single 6-cylinder Clark-Sulzer turbo charged oil engine the ships had a design speed of 17 knots. Manchester Liners meantime had withdrawn its passenger berths aboard the older turbine steamers in the face of rising costs and competition from the air. Consequently, the new ships were the first large vessels for many years to be built for the Company with no passenger accommodation although berths were still available on the older motor ships.

The **Manchester Commerce** was the first to be delivered and she loaded at Manchester in July 1963 for the Great Lakes. She was a huge improvement on the old turbine steamers and put the relatively new **Manchester Miller** completely in the shadow. Commodore Fred Downing had assumed his position aboard the **Manchester Miller** in 1961 following the retirement of his brother Commodore William Downing. The brothers had joined Manchester Liners together as apprentices in 1913.

The **Manchester Commerce** had five main holds and 'tween decks with additional 'tween deck space beneath the poop where there was also a small hold. She was the first of the big engines and bridge aft ships in the fleet and to help navigation in the Ship Canal and in the St Lawrence Seaway was equipped with closed circuit television fixed to the bows. At last the helmsman could see the forward tug. When she left Middlesbrough there were two more ships of the same design on the stocks: the **Manchester Renown** which was launched at the end of October and the **Manchester City** which was launched the following spring.

On 15 April 1964, just before the launch of the **Manchester City**, the **Manchester Renown** sailed under Captain W G Oliver from Eastham on her maiden voyage. Shortly afterwards in July, Captain J T Jones took the **Manchester City** down the Mersey on her maiden voyage. The deployment of the three new ships allowed the older turbine steamers to be weeded out. First to go was the wartime-built **Manchester Trader** which had begun to require costly structural maintenance to maintain her in class. She was sold for demolition following the delivery of the **Manchester Commerce** in 1963. The following year the next two new ships displaced the **Manchester Port** and **Manchester City**, being the oldest of the **Manchester Port**-type turbine steamers. Sad though it was to see these old ships sailing to the breaker's yards they were thoroughly outdated, inefficient and were no longer suited to the trade on offer.

The **Manchester Commerce** (1963) below Barton High Level Bridge outbound on 7 April 1968.

[Author]

The **Manchester City** (1964) below Irwell Park Wharf, outbound on 28 February 1965.

[Author]

The **Manchester Trader** was delivered to a shipbreaking beach in Yugoslavia by Captain John McLaren. Captain McLaren had only just recovered from the ignominy of grounding the **Manchester City** in the Cape Fear River at Wilmington, NC. Armed with that experience he was now charged with running the

Manchester Trader straight at the beach at full speed. The ship shuddered as she hit the ground and slithered up the beach to a halt. Before the insurance wire could be made fast the lightly ballasted vessel shuddered once more and slowly and inevitably slipped down the beach whence she had come to float once again in deep water. The Captain muttered something about 'When I try to put a ship aground I can't do it…', but after lining the ship up for a second attempt he was better rewarded. Crew and officers later left their charge for a five star hotel in Zagreb without a tear for the old lady.

The **Western Prince** had now thoroughly served her apprenticeship and so the Prince of Wales feathers was taken down from the funnel and the ship repainted in full ML colours. A plate was tack welded over the name, which now read **Manchester Trader**. She was again joined by her Prince Line consort the **Southern Prince**, but only seasonally. The **Western Prince** was not averse to new colours, having served on charter to the Brocklebank Line in the late 1950s and then as the **Zealandic** in Shaw Savill's livery.

The **Western Prince** in ML colours as the **Manchester Trader** (1955) outbound above Runcorn on 10 July 1966.

[Author]

Seasonal winter use of the **Manchester Faith** and **Manchester Fame** on Yeoward Line's Canary Island fruit runs came to an end in 1964. The Spanish Government decreased the travel time for the fruit by just one day and this disqualified any ships that could not attain 16 knots. As it happened the Cairn Line were struggling to fill their relatively big ships on the north-east England and Leith for Canada service and an inter-Furness Withy group swap was arranged. The smaller **Manchester Faith** and **Manchester Fame** became the **Cairnesk** and **Cairnglen** while the larger Cairn Line ships, the steamer **Cairngowan** and motor ship **Cairnforth**, transferred to Manchester Liners as the **Manchester Engineer** and **Manchester Freighter** respectively. The four ships reverted to their former names when they were swapped back to their rightful owners in 1966. In addition the steamer **Cairndhu** was bought outright by Manchester Liners and given the name **Manchester Exporter**.

The deployment of the three Cairn Line ships provided a valuable stop-gap which allowed trade to develop without the Company being over-reliant on the vagaries of the charter market. However, none of the ships was ideal for the trade on offer in the mid-1960s, so rapidly had developments taken place since the opening of the St Lawrence Seaway in 1959.

The Glasgow-based Donaldson Line had made a deal with the Cairn Line to share the Canadian whisky import trade through Glasgow rather than Leith so allowing the Cairn Line into the Clyde. This privilege was ceded to Manchester Liners in 1966 so allowing the Company berthing rights in the Glasgow Conference for the first time.

Cairn Line's **Cairndhu** (1952) was brought by ML and renamed **Manchester Exporter**.

[Author's collection]

The **Manchester Exporter** (1952) inbound below Irlam locks in March 1966.

[Author]

But life was not all good and the national seamen's strike between 16 May and 1 July severely stressed Company operations. It coincided with a strike of the lock keepers in the St Lawrence Seaway and a dockers' strike in Montreal. Although the **Manchester Merchant** managed to sail from Manchester on 15 May she became strike bound at Montreal until the end of July, while the **Manchester Freighter** sat fully crewed at Toronto for 38 days also earning nothing for her owners. To help keep the goods moving the Royal Mail Lines' motor ship **Escalante** dating from 1955 was bareboat chartered for several round trips across the Atlantic.

One of the key developments taking place at that time was various experiments with packaged goods. Collapsible wooden containers had been in use for some time to allow cars and furniture to be stacked in the hold three and four boxes high. This developed into palletised goods and then 8 foot square boxes, and subsequently 10 foot square boxes were introduced. However, there was a limit to size and weight because the cargo handling gear could not cope with anything larger and heavier. The move was towards the standard 8 x 8 x 20 foot container which provided far more flexibiity than the smaller company boxes. Demand was greatest from Chicago and to cope with this the **Manchester Shipper** was fitted with a single 30 ton derrick so that the large American containers started to come to Manchester. The dockers managed some awful damage with the containers, at both ends of the journey, and single derrick handling was clearly not going to be the optimum method forever. The experiment was driven by US Customs who looked kindly on the container plus the declining productivity of the Canadian services due to the port delays caused by industrial unrest on both sides of the Atlantic. While ISO standards were being worked on to provide an international and intermodal standard 20 foot container, Manchester Liners was right in there at the start.

The chartered **Manchester Engineer** (1952) proudly retaining Newcastle as her port of registry.

[John Clarkson]

The **Manchester Freighter** (1958), outbound below Irwell Park Wharf in January 1967, was also on charter from the Cairn Line.

[Author]

One of the biggest drawbacks of the twenty foot container was that it had a weight limit. Although this was not a problem for British exports it was a significant issue for the imports where 30 tons of metal or bulk goods only partly filled the container. The answer was the split half height container which could be loaded aboard the **Manchester Shipper** using her own gear yet stacked one above the other in the hold as if they were a single container.

At the 68th Annual General Meeting in 1966 Kenneth Stoker reported:

We are the first British company to start in a modest way a container service to Chicago in conjunction with a new Customs-approved container clearing depot in Manchester. From our limited experience in this field we realise that much more careful study, research and experiment will be needed before a full appreciation can be gained.

Two further ships were built at Smith's Dock for the Company and delivered in November 1966 and February 1967. These were the so called 'container friendly' ships **Manchester Port** and **Manchester Progress**, each equipped with a 30 ton deck crane and the normal array of lighter derricks and cranes. The ships were capable of handling both the standard 20 foot container and still carry the traditional break-bulk cargoes on which Manchester Liners had so long relied. They were powered by the new style French Pielstick engines built under licence by Crossley Premier Engines at its works in Openshaw. New ships they might be, but dockers' disputes coupled with weather and ice delays caused the **Manchester Progress**, although ice strengthened, to take an incredible 90 days over her second return voyage. For much of this time she was held at Quebec by the dockers, neither unloaded nor loaded. The previous year the **Southern Prince**, again on charter to ML, had taken 86 days over a similar trip.

The **Manchester Port** (1966) outbound at Barton on 10 January 1969.

[Author]

The new pair of ships also realised a totally new concept, that of all year round navigation to ice-bound Montreal. The ice-strengthened ships of J Lauritzen of Denmark had been used to introduce winter sailings to Montreal in 1964. This had become possible as Government ice breakers had been deployed to prevent flooding above Quebec. Lauritzen had been quick to work alongside this development and were reaping a handsome profit. Robert Stoker put it succinctly 'A Scandinavian company had been running a winter service to Montreal for two to three years – that is why we had to go in. We do not want them to take all our traffic.' Manchester Liners response was modification of the original design of the two new sisters by upgrading the vessels' hulls to ice strengthened class so allowing a through winter service to Montreal rather than diverting to St John. Additional innovation was the provision of bridge controls for the twin Pielstick oil engines, so allowing the engine rooms to be unmanned during the night watches - these were ships of an altogether new pedigree.

The new ships displaced the pre-war built **Manchester Progress** to the shipbreakers in January 1966 and placed the 1951-completed **Manchester Merchant** on the For Sale list the following year. Although the **Manchester Merchant** was the youngest of the Blythswood-built **Manchester Port**-type steamers, she was developing severe corrosion problems which reflected the poor quality steel available in the postwar years. Nonetheless she found a buyer and traded under the Liberian flag of convenience for several years until lost to fire on a voyage between Chittagong and Rotterdam in February 1972. The rapid changeover from steam ship to motor ship meant that a number of greatly experienced steam certificated engineer officers had either to retrain or leave, while experienced motor engineers were brought anew into the Company. As it happened, a number of the 'steamers' were approaching retirement age and were happy to go ashore early.

The **Manchester Regiment** and the older war-built **Manchester Shipper** remained in the Manchester Liners fleet as the last of the Blythswood-built steamers, the **Manchester Shipper**, of course, now being an 'ultra modern container ship'. Both ships adopted the pale green hull colour of the Lakers in order to keep hold temperatures down in the summer, as earlier the old **Manchester City** had also been greened up for the Lakes. Decks were covered in aluminium paint to assist in reflecting the sun's energy and resort was also made to spraying the decks with water while in the lakes when lard and edible oils were aboard! Although the pair still remained in the fleet, their tenure could not be prolonged while the rust streaks on the green hulls became ever more prominent. The **Manchester Regiment** went to pastures new in 1967 and the **Manchester Shipper** took her thirty ton container derrick to an Italian breaker's yard two summers later.

The container-friendly ship **Manchester Shipper** (1943) above Barton in April 1962 complete with Great Lakes green hull.

[Author]

Links with Irish Shipping were strengthened in 1967 when the **Irish Spruce** and **Irish Poplar**, both with large refrigerated space, were put into a joint Manchester and Dublin to USA service with Manchester Liners calling at Dublin to service the old Irish Shipping connection to Canada. This arrangement survived into the early 1970s. A similar liaison with Charles Hill's Bristol City Line to run between Bristol Channel ports and Manchester to the USA was less successful and lasted only one season. This failed largely because of ongoing labour disputes at the ports, notably Avonmouth.

There was trouble aboard the **Manchester Exporter** in August 1967 with twelve passengers aboard. Drums of sodium peroxide had spilled in the hold igniting combustible material causing an explosion which ripped off the after hatch. The ship was 450 miles off the Irish coast but fortunately both the **Manchester Merchant** and **Manchester Fame** were nearby and were able to stand by the **Manchester Exporter** while her crew fought the flames wearing fire helmets and breathing masks to protect them from the chemical fumes. The fire was successfully dowsed and the ship was able to proceed under her own power to Belfast. Sadly one of her crew died during the emergency when men on the poop had to crawl beneath the fire through the emergency tunnel to get to the central part of the ship.

A similar problem had earlier befallen the **Manchester Merchant** when fire developed in bales of nylon, filling the hold with toxic fumes. Again the crew were able to bring the blaze under control using breathing apparatus, although at one stage it looked as if the fire would get to the oil fuel bunkers. In this case the ship was able to make her way safely to Halifax without casualty.

Another chemical fire occurred when the **Manchester Miller** was in New York loading chemicals in 1968. This fire was put out by 200 firemen with 42 fire engines, two fire tenders and several tugs. With the weight of water pumped into the ship she slowly settled on the bottom with a 7° list. Raised and patched up, she was brought home for permanent repairs. Her main crew accommodation had been gutted but was not replaced and thereafter many of the engineering department staff enjoyed the comparative luxury of the former passenger cabins. However, passenger berths were still available aboard the **Manchester Spinner** and **Manchester Mariner** and the former Cairn Line ships.

A new company called the Manchester Prince Line was set up in 1968 to trade with the Mediterranean. The Prince Line, part of the Furness Withy group, had run its Mediterranean service from both Manchester and London. Both routes were losing money and Manchester Liners agreed to take on the Manchester end of the business, buying the Prince Line loading brokers Gough & Crosthwaite and paying £10,000 for the right to join the Mediterranean west coast UK Conference. Three small cargo ships were taken on charter in 1968: Coast Lines' **Lancashire Coast** and **Cheshire Coast** were given the names **Trojan Prince** and **Spartan Prince** for much of the year and the British & Continental Steamship Company's **Egret** became the **Tartar Prince** until 1971. These replaced the rather stately Prince Line vessels which had over-generous yacht-like passenger accommodation at the expense of deadweight.

Manchester Prince Line's **Tartar Prince** (1959) was chartered from the British & Continental Steamship Company. Formerly the **Egret** she was sold when the ML charter ended in 1971.

[Author's collection]

A problem with return cargoes from the Mediterranean was overcome by the additional purchase of the Golden Cross Line and Constantine Lines which also gave access to new trading opportunities although calls at Italian ports ceased shortly afterwards. Constantine Lines had the small motor ships **Gartwood** and **Lochwood**, each with first class accommodation for twelve passengers, and latterly the **Eastwood**, running down to the Mediterranean in collaboration with the **Gracechurch** which was owned by the Coquet Shipping Company of Middlesbrough and principally serving Libyan ports. Collectively they traded as the Gracechurch Line which until 1952 had been known as the Golden Cross Line. It was Golden Cross Line, which was still owned by the Coquet company managers Anthony & Bainbridge, along with Constantine Lines that ML purchased. The **Eastwood** was retained by the Constantine Shipping Company, which continued to trade as such, and the **Gracechurch** was retained by the Coquet company. ML, therefore, bought expertise and local knowledge, agents and clients.

The **Trojan Prince** (1954), outbound below Barton Locks, was chartered from Coast Lines in 1968.

[Author]

Typical of the Prince Line 'yachting' image was the **Norman Prince** (1956), seen here below Barton in July 1966.

[Author's collection]

Manchester Liners continued the year with further acquisitions in order to service its diverse needs. Robert Stoker wrote in *Sea Breezes* November 1984:

The ship repair firm of Morrell Mills & Company Ltd - the second oldest firm in Trafford Park having been founded in 1899 – was taken over, one of the subsidiaries being the old established ship's caterers and provision merchants James Walker & Son (Shipping) Ltd, founded in 1865. A further acquisition at that time was that of Condrons (Manchester) Ltd, boilers scalers and cleaners since 1910.

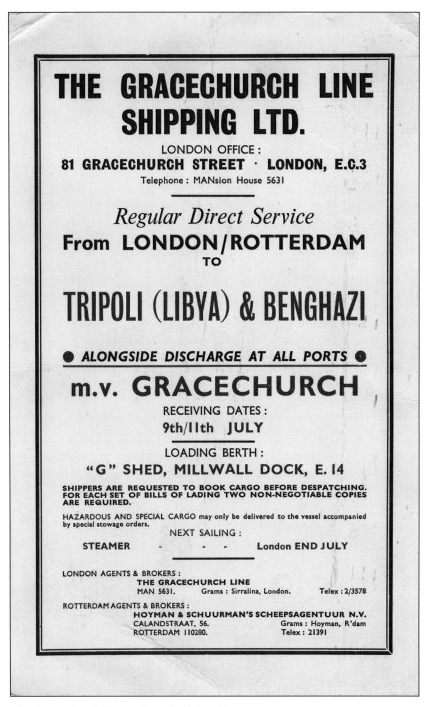

The Gracechurch Line: advert for July 1962.

Two more friends departed in 1968, their services overtaken by the new motor ships. The **Manchester Spinner** and **Manchester Mariner** were sold to Stravelakis Brothers and put under the Greek flag. Sadly, the former sank following an engine room explosion in November 1971, though the **Manchester Mariner** survived in trade until she was broken up in 1977. The former Cairn Line steamer **Manchester Exporter** was also sold to Greek owners a year later. The **Manchester Faith** and **Manchester Fame** survived until 1970, partly on charter work, and were sold to Liberian flag owners, although temporarily chartered back to ML (see Chapter 10), with both surviving well into the 1980s.

Manchester and Canada had together come a long way since the war years. Manchester's rebuilding continued apace, the CIS Tower, Piccadilly Plaza, the Arndale Centre and Gateway House at Piccadilly Station were just some of the buildings completed in the 1960s. But all in all, on both sides of the Atlantic, the early 1960s were boom years for all to enjoy and Manchester Liners had ridden that boom to its full extent. But times were changing and needs must, both Manchester and its Liners were set to change, and change fast.

THE SHORE GANG - BASED ON AN ARTICLE BY PETER FRIER
(http://www.manchesterliners.co.uk/oldnews2004.htm)

In 1960 Captain Whitby became Marine Superintendent and Chief Officer Peter Frier came ashore to look after the Manchester Shore Gang. The Shore Gang comprised a team of about thirty men including ABs, bosuns and various specialists such as a storekeeper, messman and carpenter. There were two foremen, confusingly named Jim Mouat at No 8 Dock Office and Jim Mowat in the mess room at No 9 Dock, and always referred to as 'Wilmslow' Mouat and 'Corky' Mowat. These were the men that took over from the crew of the ships as they arrived at Manchester, so that the sea-going staff could take shore leave. Duties including shifting ship as required, cleaning and painting, taking on stores and a host of other duties. Whenever the Superintendent was seen striding down the quay the letter W for Whitby was made with two hands so that everybody had time to look busy and workman-like, and even the officers had time to wake up and look attentive out on deck!

*The worst job that fell to the Shore Gang was digging out the liquid lard tanks to get the residue into the pumps and then cleaning the tanks. It also fell to the Shore Gang to recover the painting scow submerged under the stern of the **Manchester Shipper** when she started testing engines. Like clockwork, the 60-ton floating crane was brought across and the steel scow was lifted onto the quayside before anyone noticed anything was amiss. But the highlight of the year was always the annual outing. A bus was hired and they would set out for the Cheshire countryside - and a pub. Anyone senior enough could come so long as they were not from the St Ann's Square Office!*

But the days when the ships shut down the generators overnight leaving a watchman with an oil stove and light were long gone. The coming of the big motor ships required little from the Shore Gang and the team was slowly run down and all but gone by the early 1970s.

The **Manchester Shipper**, again with seagoing crew, heads down the Manchester Ship Canal.

[Author]

THE MANCHESTER CHALLENGE - THE CONTAINER REVOLUTON

The concept of the box or container to package goods together for doorstep collection and delivery was not new. First introduced in the UK by the railways, it soon gathered momentum when coastal shipping companies such as the General Steam Navigation Company and David MacBrayne adopted the scheme. In the 1950s the Americans took it up on a larger scale when the Sea-Land and Waterman companies started container carrying on the North American coastal trade using converted C2 and later T3 wartime standard tankers. Some of the early vessels carried gantry cranes for loading and unloading as shore-side facilities were not then available. The Waterman company converted its wartime-built break bulk cargo ship *Fairland* into a part cellular container ship and tried her on Transatlantic duties. It was not a commercially successful experiment, largely because there was then no standard container (the 20 foot equivalent unit (TEU) was yet to be internationally agreed), no pool of containers and no dock facilities to service loading and unloading. The experiment did, however, provide proof of concept.

Britain's first container ships were the railway-owned *Container Venturer* and *Container Enterprise*, which took up the overnight service between Belfast and Heysham in 1958. Each port was specially equipped with a single sheerlegs crane to transfer the containers to and from the ship. They were a huge success, being capable of transporting 65 Type 'B' large railway containers. The containers could be lifted from ship to rail flat and then if necessary to road flat although loading and unloading was slow because every other container had to be slid sideways before it could be craned on or off the ships.

These developments clearly had an impact on the Board of Manchester Liners where a vision of the future had become firmly embedded. But it was early days in the container industry and the capital required to enter it was such that consortia were clearly a preferred means of distributing the risk. Besides, capital was also required to install container handling facilities at ports, and a bank of containers needed to be constructed along with specialist flatbed lorries for road transport. But worse, these were the days of converted vessels, and nobody had yet set about designing the first generation cellular container ship – the stakes were indeed high.

At a meeting in 1967 the Manchester Liners' Board made the extraordinary and extremely bold and brave move to go wholly into containers. It did this in the knowledge that it would have to be instrumental in developing suitable tonnage, that it would have to work with terminal ports to develop container handling facilities and that it would need to sell the new service to its customers, old and potentially new. Indeed the marketing department both in Europe and North America had already been busy sounding out the needs of customers and had established that there was a growing demand for packaged units of cargo that could be transported door-to-door across the Atlantic. The Board recognised that transhipment of containers by rail from the dockside would greatly enhance the traditional hinterland so enabling containerised goods from, for example, Southampton to ship through Manchester with destinations virtually anywhere on the Canadian rail network. From the outset it was decided that a three or four ship service would operate a 5 to 7 day departure between Manchester and Montreal all year round.

Others were also pursuing the same vision. On the North Atlantic, the Atlantic Container Line was created in 1965 by a consortium represented in the UK by Cunard, with Compagnie Générale Maritime from France, the Dutch Brostrom Group, and Rederi A/B Transatlantic and Wallenius Rederiena both from Sweden. Four 700 TEU 'G1' (first generation) class ships were delivered to the company in 1967 led by the pioneer motor ship *Atlantic Span*, and within three years Cunard had the fast 24 knot turbine steamers *Atlantic Conveyor* and *Atlantic Causeway* registered under their name and running out of Liverpool.

All these pioneer cellular container ships doubled as roll-on roll-off vessels with a large hold aft for the stowage of trailers and other wheeled vehicles, uncontainerised palleted goods and the like. The hold was accessed by a simple linkspan hinged over the transom stern of the ships. UK terminals were Southampton and Liverpool principally for New York and other east coast US ports. This operation had little competitive interference with Manchester Liners' proposals.

The Cunard Steamship Company's **Atlantic Causeway** (1969), seen at Southampton in March 1970, was a first generation container ship in the Atlantic Container Line consortium.

[Author]

In 1965 Furness Withy became a founder member of OCL (Overseas Containers Ltd) along with British & Commonwealth Shipping (Clan Line), P&O and Ocean Steamship Company (Blue Funnel). The consortium ordered six steam turbine driven cellular container ships (later converted to motor ships), the first of which, the **Encounter Bay** inaugurated a service between UK and European ports to Australia in March 1969. The service was slow to develop and the consortium had to withstand considerable losses in the early years before OCL became a brand leader in the 1970s.

OCL's innovative cellular container ship **Encounter Bay** (1969) seen after conversion from steam to motor ship with massive funnel extension.

[Author's collection]

Containerisation was the new technology. By 1969 there were 200 container ships, large and small, under construction around the world of which 47 were designed to accommodate more than 1,000 TEUs. OCL's **Encounter Bay** was a landmark amongst these orders. The TEU or Twenty Foot Equivalent Unit had become adopted as the international standard for containers and remains the basic container unit, being some 20 feet by 8 feet wide by 8.5 feet high. Containers also come as 30 feet lengths (1.5 TEUs) and 40 feet (2 TEUs). One naval architect was heard to comment contentedly 'for the first time in dry cargo ship design the nature of the cargo was precisely known'.

Brian J Cudahy described the emerging industry in *Box Boats: How Container Ships Changed The World*:

*In addition to new container-carrying services inaugurated by ACL and OCL in the years after **Fairland**'s inaugural transatlantic voyage in 1966, two traditional European steamship companies began operating container ships between Europe and North America. Hapag-Lloyd entered the trade in 1968. Hapag-Lloyd would grow into one of the world's major container ship operators in subsequent years, and at various times would be able to boast that its fleet included the world's largest container carrying vessel. A second European steamship company to have an early presence in the North Atlantic container trade was Manchester Liners Limited... In November 1968 the company's 452 TEU **Manchester Challenge** became Great Britain's first fully cellular container ship designed for deep water trade.*

Not only was a new class of ship designed financed and built, but so too were 10,000 containers to a variety of designs. The total capital investment amounted to some £16 million. In addition port facilities had to be constructed and road haulage companies taken on board. The Monopolies and Mergers Commission report (1976) – see Chapter 11 - looking back over the history of the operation reported:

ML decided that the greatest efficiency would be obtained if it had control of its container terminals on either side of the North Atlantic, at Manchester and Montreal. In 1968 ML entered into an agreement with the Manchester Ship Canal Company which agreed to lease part of the Port of Manchester sufficiently large for all the ground facilities, the container stacking areas and roads needed for a container terminal. ML agreed to defray, over a period of 13 years, the cost of most of the equipment such as gantry cranes and straddle carriers. The total cost so far had been of the order of £2 million. The annual payments are currently of the order of £165,000. Under the arrangement which was intended to last until 1984, the Ship Canal Company reserves the container facility for ML exclusively, and ML should maintain a weekly service between Manchester and Montreal....

At Montreal ML entered into a 25 year lease for the terminal area and bore the cost of the container cranes, buildings and equipment. Special cranes and containers had to be designed for use in the winter conditions experienced in Canada.

ML's container service was immediately successful. ML then started to expand its base by purchasing a number of haulage and warehousing companies in the Manchester area, Scotland and the Northeast of England... ML also took over many of Furness Withy's operations in Canada connected with this type of business. In 1970 ML introduced what is known as its 'Flying Fish' service in which ML's containerised sea service is linked to air carriage at either end or both, thereby providing a service which is faster than an 'all surface' but cheaper than an 'all air' service.

The Montreal terminal included a covered container handling building, the terminal being located at the very end of the new trans-Atlantic Expressway.

The new ships were built by Smith's Dock Company at Middlesbrough. They had similar engines to the **Manchester Port** and **Manchester Progress**, but greater power. The two 9-cylinder Vee-type Pielstick engines coupled to a single shaft and a controllable pitch propeller provided a design speed of 19.5 knots. The ships were ice-strengthened to Lloyds Class 1 with ice protection guards around the propeller. The launch of the **Manchester Challenge**, the first of the trio, was reported in *The Guardian* 12 June 1968:

*The first ocean-going container ship built in Britain was launched at the Teesside yard of Smith's Dock Company yesterday. It is the first of three 12,000 ton deadweight ships which the yard is building for Manchester Liners... Manchester Liner's order worth £10 million included 4,500 containers which are being made by a subcontractor. The **Manchester Challenge** was launched by Mrs W G Edmunds, wife of the Managing Director.*

Andrew Bell described some of the detail within the **Manchester Challenge** and her two sisters in an article that first appeared in *Sea Breezes*, February 2011:

Two 20 feet containers of stores were loaded and stowed through their own hatch located just ahead of the accommodation block... Under the Upper Deck and running the length of the ship on the outboard side was a working alleyway to starboard and a pipe and cable one to port. There was no need to brave the weather by going on deck to reach the forecastle where the mooring arrangements were located under the forecastle head. If there was a snowstorm in Montreal's winter the mooring equipment and the windlass did not need to be excavated before use.

In its time the accommodation for a crew of only 27 was lavish, with all the officers and POs having cabins each with its own shower and toilet. A large saloon and bar area for the officers took up the whole width of the ship at Upper Deck level. All the ratings had single berth cabins and all the accommodation was air conditioned. There was an owner's suite on the Bridge Deck. The three sisters may have been the only ones ever to have provided the Radio Officer with a separate bedroom and a day room both adjacent to the radio room on the Boat Deck; his only neighbour was the master with an even larger suite.

The **Manchester Challenge** (1968), outbound above Latchford Locks on 31 August 1973.

[Author]

The **Manchester Challenge** sailed on her maiden voyage in November under Captain Phillip Fielding. On her second voyage, under Captain D G Thomas, the **Manchester Challenge** entered Montreal harbour through the winter ice, unloaded and loaded again for Manchester to depart in less than two days turn round. The ice was such that several conventional vessels were unable to sail until the following month. Her sisters, the **Manchester Courage** and **Manchester Concorde**, were delivered in February and May 1969 and the new service began in earnest. The livery of the ships was completely new. The hulls were painted in ML orange-red, with crimson boot topping and the usual wording MANCHESTER LINERS along the side. They were indeed an impressive sight especially when viewed at close quarters passing beneath one of the Ship Canal bridges.

Crossley Pielstick engines at work on board the **Manchester Challenge**.

[Rodney Hall]

With all this activity and a greatly increased head office staff, offering all kinds of new and very different expertise, St Anne's Square was forsaken for new purpose-built offices. The new Manchester Liners House was built on the old railway siding between the heads of No. 8 and No. 9 Docks in Salford, a short walk from the container terminal at the Mode Wheel end of the north-west quay of No. 9 Dock. In addition to the new 10 storey office complex, the site also included parking for 250 cars, a self service petrol station, called the Maple Leaf Garage, and a new customs hall. A 32 foot Canadian Indian totem pole greeted visitors entering the office and a polar bear fighting a sea monster overlooked the reception area. Indeed, the complex was officially opened, or rather launched, by the High Commissioner for Canada who swung a bottle of champagne onto a front pillar.

The maiden voyage of the **Manchester Courage** was successfully completed and she sailed from Salford on her second trip on 16 March. Engine problems delayed her departure from No. 9 Dock and held up the departure of the **Governor** that was to follow down the Canal. That evening the **Manchester Courage** had managed to get down to Irlam Lock with the Harrison liner hard on her heels, when the hydraulic system controlling the pitch on the propeller failed and the variable pitch propeller automatically assumed its default position in forward thrust mode. With the stern tug already let go for passage into the adjacent small lock the new ship inevitably hit the downstream gate. The force of the impact was such that the integrity of the gate was breached. It was not feasible to close the upstream gate with the flow of water passing down the lock and the level of the canal was lowered all the way back to Barton Lock. Fortunately the **Governor** was still safely above Barton. *The Guardian* 18 March 1969 reported:

*The Port of Manchester will be cut off from the sea for 6 to 8 weeks while repairs are made at Irlam Lock on the damage caused on Sunday night by the container ship **Manchester Courage**. She rammed the lock gates, wedging herself in the lock, and bottling fifteen other ships in port... Between 100 and 150 workers are to be brought in for repairs. The first task is to move the ship which is hard against the masonry of the lock sides. Then the broken lock gates will be replaced with spares. Ships drawing less than 9 or 10 feet of water may be able to bypass the blockage by using a smaller parallel lock... It had lowered the water level by 10 feet from Irlam to Barton Locks.*

The **Manchester Courage** ended up half in and half out of the lock. When she was removed and inspected it was found that the hull was undamaged but she remained trapped in the Canal until the new gates could be installed and the Canal level reinstated. This took a further five weeks, during which time the **Manchester Challenge** diverted to Liverpool and the cargo aboard the **Manchester Courage** was off-loaded with a giant crane and sent on trucks to Liverpool to join the hastily-chartered cellular container vessel **Hother Isle** which just had time to receive Manchester Liners funnel colours before sailing. For the duration of the closure the Manchester Liners flag was seen also at Barrow, Glasgow and even Hull.

The **Manchester Courage** (1969) has just sailed beneath Warburton High Level Bridge, outbound on 29 October 1970.

[Author]

The **Manchester Courage** passes the Barton bridges outbound.

[Manchester Liners Old Shipmates Association]

A tug strike in the closing months of 1969 at Manchester caused little impact to the container service as ships diverted to Greenock and their containers were discharged and assembled for departure with almost no delay.

Early container competition from subsidised US carriers including Sea-Land, with its fast 30 knot, but fuel-demanding, twin screw steam turbine ships of the S-L7 class, had rapidly undermined the profits of the Donaldson Line and Canadian Pacific working out of the Clyde, and amalgamations were sought. In March 1970 Manchester Liners started to call at the Greenock container terminal in collaboration with Canadian Pacific and what had become Head-Donaldson, Manchester Liners acting very much as 'the son of the Cairn Line'. The new rationalised service allowed a weekly sailing from the Clyde under the local management of the Donaldson Line. The inaugural sailing was by the Head-Donaldson Lines' **Inishowen Head** (8,621 gross tons), following a four month long conversion from conventional general cargo to cellular container ship (350 TEU).

As it happened, one of the first victims of the success of the new container services turned out to be the Dalgleish service to Churchill, the Dalgleish company ceasing to trade from 1970.

During 1970 the steamer **Manchester Miller** was taken in hand at Smith's Dock for conversion into a fully cellular container ship. Just why the **Manchester Miller** was chosen for conversion remains unclear, although she had always been something of a misplaced favourite of the Board. The appearance of the vessel was completely changed with high container platforms fore and aft and the forward deck raised to forecastle level. An odd looking craft indeed, now renamed **Manchester Quest**, she still retained her curved fronted bridge structure amidships. Just what the Board planned for her each winter when the St Lawrence iced up was unclear, but their faith in steam turbines and tolerance of plentiful dead space in the holds suggested a desperation to expand the cellular tonnage to which it had access.

The conversion of the **Manchester Miller** was clearly considered cost effective by the Board, and the **Manchester Progress**, which had an ice-strengthened hull and whose hold at least conformed to ISO container measurements, was dispatched to Amsterdam in 1971 for similar treatment. She returned as the red-hulled container ship **Manchester Concept**, with her forward well plated over to make a flush deck. She at least looked like a container ship. Her sister, the **Manchester Port**, was sold, as also were the three sisters **Manchester Commerce**, **Manchester City** and **Manchester Renown**, Manchester Liners being wholly committed to the container on its transatlantic service.

Three photographs which illustrate the way that Manchester Liners began to adapt to containerisation.

The **Manchester Progress** (1967) as built and seen off Eastham.

[John Clarkson]

Now converted and renamed **Manchester Concept** she bears little resemblance to her original appearance.

[Author's collection]

The container ship **Manchester Quest** (1959) was formerly the break bulk **Manchester Miller**.

[John Clarkson]

A conventional general cargo service was maintained in parallel with the container service, using largely chartered vessels. For example in the summer of 1970 the former **Manchester Faith** and **Manchester Fame** sailed again under the ML flag as the **Ilkon Tak** and **Ilkon Niki** respectively, working alongside the American freighter **Helen Miller** and the smaller **Sally Isle**.

During the year the subsidiary company Cargo Airships Limited was established with offices in Manchester and London. The company was run by Max Rhynish, a staunch protagonist of the airship concept and an aviation writer; it had a staff of two. The objective was to study the potential for cargo airships and Rhynish enthusiastically stated in a press bulletin 'Eventually, nuclear power could drive the airship but diesel electric power was much more likely in the early days. The capacity could be ten times that of a big modern cargo aeroplane'.

Chairman Robert Stoker reported a buoyant year to his shareholders in the October 1970 AGM referring to the fleet of dedicated container lorries the company now operated as well as the Flying Fish onward connection by air for palletised cargo:

The container service between Manchester and Montreal was in excellent shape and the other container services had come up to expectations. The group's road haulage venture had proved thoroughly satisfactory and the Flying Fish service was flying higher each day.

The break-bulk service to Chicago was replaced by a Lakes feeder service to Montreal during the open-water season. This was started during 1971 by two small chartered vessels named **Manchester Mercurio** and **Manchester Rapido**, which as their non-traditional names suggest were registered in Spain. The new **Manchester Merit** spent the start of her commercial life in the Lakes until chartered ships arrived. A weekly train charter ran between Montreal and Toronto, with Hamilton, Chicago, Detroit and Winnipeg connected to Montreal either by road or rail.

The **Manchester Rapido** (1971) was a chartered vessel.

[Fotoflite incorporating Skyfotos]

The small container ship **Manchester Merit** (1970) was intended for Great Lakes feeder service in summer and the Mediterranean routes in winter.

[Author's collection]

The **Manchester Merit** was a 3,400 ton cellular container ship designed to introduce container carrying to the Mediterranean for the Manchester Prince Line. Built in Spain she first visited the Mediterranean on charter to the Spanish company Contemar, but later sailed for the Manchester Prince Line. Contemar was a useful contact as it provided a valuable feeder service to the Manchester to Montreal container ships. The **Manchester Merit** remained in Manchester Liners' colours only until 1972 when she was demise chartered to Bermudan owners and renamed **Fortuna** and retained under charter for the lakes feeder services for Manchester Liners.

The success of the big cellular container ships can only be judged by the ordering of a further identical sister, the **Manchester Crusade**. She was delivered by Smith's Dock in March 1971. The finance for both this ship and the earlier **Manchester Concorde** was provided by the Industrial and Commercial Finance Corporation and both ships were registered under the ownership of its subsidiary the Nile Steamship Company of London and demise chartered to Manchester Liners. The success of this class of ship is illustrated by the statistic that on completion of her 100th round trip to Montreal in 1975, the **Manchester Challenge** had lifted 95,000 containers weighing just short of 11.5 million tons and had sailed some 554,000 miles through all weathers and ice conditions.

But despite the new fleet being ice-strengthened, damage and delays still occurred. The **Manchester Concept** sailed in ice from Montreal on one occasion late in 1972 and was ordered to stand by the **Manchester Crusade** in the Gulf of St Lawrence. The **Manchester Crusade** had suffered rudder damage from floating ice while approaching the Gulf and her steering had become difficult and unpredictable. The stern anchor of the **Manchester Concept** was lifted on deck using the light aft derrick, and the anchor unshackled. Using a leading line the anchor chain was transferred to the port bow of the **Manchester Crusade** and made fast. The vessel was successfully 'steered' into Sept Iles Bay and handed over to tugs. Now being canny fellows, the crew of the **Manchester Concept**, wholly owned by Manchester Liners, determined they warranted a salvage reward for rescuing the **Manchester Crusade** managed by Manchester Liners but owned by the Nile Shipping Company. Their cheek was rewarded by a small bonus paid to crew members the following month!

The **Manchester Concept** (1967) was formerly the **Manchester Progress**. She is seen at the container terminal in Manchester.

[Bernard McCall]

Keeping track of the containers was not easy and a card and tag system was developed to assist with this. Even so, ML once carried out a helicopter search of north-west England looking for its wayward red painted boxes, and agents in Canada and the US were forever on the lookout for cases of misuse or misappropriation. Once the former Prince Line Mediterranean service switched to containers in the early 1970s there was no chance of keeping track and Manchester Liners containers fell to all manner of uses. One pair was found in use at a customs depot in Libya, the containers being nicely wooden lined, unlike others, providing some insulation from the heat of the sun. Another was found in Turkey having been converted into a roadside teashop. Ingenuity, it seems, knew no bounds.

R B Stoker concluded from these first few years of container service in an article in *Sea Breezes* November 1984:

Exporters were finding that the new container service reduced transport time by up to 75%, cut pilferage and damage and – mainly because of under-deck stowage – reduced insurance claims by 99.5% over conventionally stowed goods. There were stabilising effects on transportation costs which would otherwise have gone up to such an extent as to have a disastrous effect on export markets.

The core of the service was a six ship twice weekly fully cellular container ship service between Manchester and Montreal crossing the Atlantic in just 6½ days. The planning and investment had certainly paid off and the company totally transformed to containers in the space of just these few years.

But there was one other vital change that had occurred in these years – the Company had been taken over. During 1970 Furness Withy determined it would buy the share capital in Manchester Liners that it did not already own. By the end of the year it held a 56% holding and Manchester Liners had finally become a subsidiary of Furness Withy. Things carried on much as before and in 1971 the Company won the Queen's Award for Industry and every ship carried the logo on the superstructure – Manchester Liners remained a very proud Company.

HARRISON LINE AND THE MANCHESTER SHIP CANAL
by Captain Michael Jones, former Marine Superintendent of the Harrison Line

During the fifties and sixties three out of the six regular homeward services operated by the Harrison Line featured the port of Manchester. The Masters, officers and crew could look forward to a short spell at home when their voyage of perhaps three or four months ended at Manchester. The Manchester Ship Canal was viewed as something which had to be endured before the pleasure of getting home but was not felt a particular problem or seen through apprehension although it was something which needed careful planning and some care and skill while in the Canal itself.

A major question was the permissible draught in the Canal. The maximum draught from the sea to Ellesmere Port was 29 feet and thence on to Manchester the maximum draught was 26 feet 6 inches in freshwater. Therefore, the ship had to arrive at Ellesmere Port, if that was the first point of discharge, at 29 feet even keel and 26 feet 6 inches even keel from there to Manchester itself. Often the trim of the ship was secured weeks earlier in ports like Beira in Mozambique with the careful distribution in the various holds of the heavy cargo, the close weight commodities, such as copper ingots and chrome ore. Get it wrong at that time and it was wrong for the whole voyage. The problem was not eased by the Harrison rule that ballast tanks were not permitted to be filled when under or adjacent to stowed cargo. However, it is not recorded that a Harrison vessel was ever unable to complete a transit of the Canal due to trim problems. When outward bound from Manchester the necessity of ensuring funnel and masts were under the height restriction of 71 feet 6 inches caused by the road and rail bridges was another matter, in particular if there was still Liverpool cargo aboard.

After the discharge of the Manchester cargo Relief Masters and officers usually took the ships down to Liverpool where any remaining cargo would be landed before commencing to load for the next voyage. On these occasions the deck ratings came from a company in Manchester who supplied gangs of ships riggers. These men knew the Ship Canal so well that between Manchester and Liverpool the Chief officer never even needed to open his mouth.

Handling the ships in the Canal itself might appear to have been a major hazard. In fact due to the skill of the Ship Canal Company tug masters and their method of securing to the ship the whole operation was made very efficient and safe. At the entrance to the Canal at Eastham tugs were made fast to the vessel at each end with two wires from each tug in the form of a very short bridle. This permitted the tugs to move from one side to another very quickly while still maintaining the strain on the wires - a great benefit when manoeuvring in the restricted spaces in the Canal and the docks. The Mersey river tugs due to having to operate in rough sea conditions used much longer wires or ropes which lost the advantage of quick reaction. This is illustrated by the fact that when moving a vessel through the Liverpool dock system a clearance of fifty feet was regarded as hazardous and necessitated much whistle blowing and men running around with fenders. But in Number 9 Dock in Manchester moving between ships berthed on either side with grain elevators and barges moored alongside them with only about two feet clearance on either side was regarded as being insignificant.

Of course the skill of the Ship Canal Pilots and their helmsmen, who were invariably trainee pilots, played a big part in the safe operation of the ships when in transit. Harrison Line, amongst others, had its own preferred pilots to the advantage of all.

In the early days, shipping traffic communications were very basic. The lock master at each lock would tell the pilot and the master what ships they would meet on the next section of the canal and a man might emerge from a canal side wooden hut, perhaps at Runcorn, and bellow into the wind some indecipherable message about the oncoming traffic.

Once inward bound, and when just starting to round the Runcorn bend under the railway bridge, a Shell tanker was encountered about to do the same thing but in the opposite direction. The skill of the pilot and the Masters of the tugs extracted both ships from this dangerous situation. This was the really clever part when two large ships passed each other when underway and going in opposite directions. This should only be done on straight sections of the Canal and used the shallow water Canal effect of pressure and suction giving attraction and repulsion to the ships and canal banks. The Master took little part in the drama as the pilot and his helmsman co-ordinated the whole thing between them from the wheelhouse with the Master on the wing of the bridge marvelling how close his ship was to the other and both ships travelling at some speed. Basically both ships steered directly for the other until they were about half a ships length apart and then both would put its rudder hand-a-starboard and the pressure and suction influence came into play as the ships became close. The bow of each ship would repel the bow of the other due to the water pressure but when the influence of the Canal bank became effective it was the skill of the pilots using the helm and the ship's engines together with the high manoeuvrability of the tugs that always enabled the large ships to pass each other in comfort and safety.

I remember also that due to the number of claims for broken ropes received from vessels moored alongside caused by excessive speed, Harrisons had a special logbook in which the condition and state of the moorings of all moored vessels had to be carefully noted.

The green fields alongside the canal and the livestock grazing in them with houses in the distance was a marvellous sight for the crews, in particular after what might have been a rough, wet and stormy passage across the Atlantic. The lady whose house was close to the canal near Chester Road swing bridge just before Latchford, who always came to her door to wave her hand at all the ships was something very welcome to all the crew. She said to us, 'You are almost home', while the younger crew members paid more attention to the girls on the balconies of the gas cooker factory at Latchford lock broadly for the same reasons.

The *Tactician* (1961) approaching Barton locks inbound to Manchester.

[Author]

CHAPTER 11

CONSOLIDATION, COMPETITION AND CHARTERING

The years 1971 and 1972 were hampered by dock workers strikes both in Manchester and Montreal. Dockers were understandably threatened by the container technology but their action did little to safeguard their own jobs. The strikes cost ML £1.5 million, the company returning a small trading loss in both years.

The small cellular container ship, **Frontier**, was delivered from her builders in Santander in 1972. The registered owner of the ship was Condrons (Manchester) Ltd. This company bought the ship following her launch and was able to advise on the fitting out of the vessel. Her Spanish-built Deutz engines gave her a handsome speed of 15 knots. On delivery she was chartered to Manchester Liners and placed on Mediterranean duties under the Manchester Prince Line banner, although she was equally suitable for service in the Lakes. Ownership by subsidiary Condrons (Manchester) attracted tax benefits and was a move to be repeated later with other vessels. The Lakes service had already been augmented by the chartered vessel **Fortuna**, formerly the **Manchester Merit** and renamed again in 1975 when she was resold to become the **Kathleen**, but still under charter to Manchester Liners.

Two medium-sized cellular container ships, the **Manchester Zeal** and **Manchester Vigour** were delivered by Appledore Shipbuilders Ltd. in Devon in summer 1973. These ships were designed primarily for the Mediterranean services but for their first two years they were variously chartered out for use in Australia, the American Gulf and on USA to Europe services. Successful charters were arranged in 1976 for the pair as the **Cargo Zeal** and **Cargo Vigour** with the Italian company Cargo Liners SA. The charterers were failing to cover costs the following year and the pair reverted to their earlier identities and were put onto the ML Mediterranean services. Other vessels, such as the 500 ton Danish-owned **Manchester Shipper** were chartered in to maintain the Mediterranean services.

The **Manchester Zeal** (1973) in the Mersey approaching Eastham on 20 March 1980.

[Laurie Schofield]

The Golden Cross Line was reactivated in 1973 as a separately identified brand to cater for Canadian cargo that could not be carried by container. Break-bulk and specialist heavy lift ships were chartered for this activity. The Company even won the Gold Headed Cane when the Canadian Chimo Shipping Company's vessel **Sir John Crosbie** entered Montreal on 1 January 1977 on Golden Cross business.

The **Manchester Vigour** (1973) outbound in the River Mersey on 2 July 1977.

[Laurie Schofield]

A report in *Sea Breezes* dated June 1973 records a significant move by Manchester Liners:

Celebrating their 75th anniversary this year, Manchester Liners has marked the occasion by widening its sphere of operations. The company opened a new container service at the end of April from Rotterdam and Felixstowe to Montreal with weekly sailings, the first sailing being taken by the container ship **Manchester Concorde**. *She was followed by sister ship* **Manchester Crusade**. *The service is complementary to the company's regular sailings from Manchester, but will be in a position to take advantage of Common Market traffic from Rotterdam. The appearance of Manchester Liners' vessels at Felixstowe adds more to the wide variety of ships to be seen at this continually growing port, and the company has opened its own office there.*

A key reason for this development was the continued industrial unrest at Manchester, and splitting the service with another port was a means of hedging bets against port closure or potential delay. Although the continental link showed great promise it was slow to develop and it was in direct competition with CP Ships, the new title adopted in 1971 for Canadian Pacific Steamships Ltd, operating from London. The two companies recognised this and went into negotiation so that in January 1974 Manchester Liners withdrew from Felixstowe and Rotterdam and CP Ships withdrew from Liverpool and Glasgow. The obvious benefit to Manchester Liners after only eight months loss making service from Rotterdam and Felixstowe was significant as CP Ships' regular clients left Liverpool for Manchester.

One homeward voyage, lasting two whole weeks, demonstrated how difficult it was to maintain schedule during the winter months. The **Manchester Courage** sailed from Montreal on 30 December 1973, only to come to a halt in thick ice above Quebec. Freedom came early the following morning with the help of two Canadian ice-breakers. Asked by Head Office to proceed on one engine due to escalating costs of fuel caused by the Yom Kippur War, the master Captain Illingworth decided to go via the northerly direct route expecting no ice. But he soon found that the ship and the containers stowed on deck were icing up and was inevitably forced to run south with both engines. Even the heated bridge windows froze over at one point reducing visibility to the small clear view screens; radar was useless as the scanners were covered in ice.

During the night the easterly course was resumed but in the morning of 3 January the **Manchester Courage**, with a following force eight gale, received a garbled message from a vessel which was on fire some 220 miles to the south-south-west. The ship turned course yet again, this time into the wind, only to learn the next day that the call letters matched a ship safely tucked up in a US port. Course for Fastnet was again resumed, two engines being needed due to the stress on the bearings from extended use of just a single engine on a shaft designed to be driven by two engines in tandem. The **Manchester Courage** eventually hove-to off Point Lynas in Anglesey on the afternoon of 11 January. The Mersey pilot was taken on board and shortly afterwards it was learnt that a southerly Force 10 was brewing so closing their entry to the Mersey and Eastham.

The **Manchester Courage** finally entered the Canal early on the morning of the 13 January and then only narrowly missing being run down by a coaster dragging her anchors. The final problem was that the container berth in No. 9 Dock was occupied and the **Manchester Courage** was ordered to wait at a berth in No. 8 Dock. But the vessel touched a shallow area and immediately sheered across the dock, the fore and aft tugs only just saving a collision with the quayside. The after tug captain reported later that the stern of the **Manchester Courage** dropped by about one foot when she touched bottom due to the reduction in buoyancy. The soft mud allowed the ship to be dragged off rapidly and refloated.

The **Manchester Crusade** was involved in a collision in the Mersey in January 1974. She received a large gash above the water line to her forepeak after colliding with the 8,200 ton Liberian flagged bulk carrier **Rhine Ore** which was holed amidships on her port side. Both vessels were repaired and soon back at work.

The **Manchester Crusade** (1971) from the air.

[Fotoflite incorporating Skyfotos]

A hostile bid for Manchester Liners took place in 1974. Eurocanadian Shipholdings' Cast company founded by Canadian Frank Narby attempted to gain the 44% of ML shares not held by Furness Withy. Cast was using bulk carriers with containers sitting on top of the cargo as a cheap non-Conference service for the less discerning shippers. But with low overheads the company had money to burn. *The Guardian* 9 October 1974 reported:

The Furness Withy shipping group said last night it was not intending to launch an offer for the 44% of shares in Manchester Liners which it does not already own. Recently the group has been buying shares in opposition to the Canadian shipping concern Eurocanadian, which is offering 85p a share for the minority stake. The [Furness] group is still not disclosing what total percentage of the Manchester Liners equity it is prepared to acquire before it stops buying at more than 85p.

Furness Withy failed to increase its holding to 75% against competition from an anonymous third party buyer situated in Manchester who at the end of 1974 held 30% of the ML shares. For the moment ML was secure from further advances from Cast.

In June 1974 Company acquisitions finally included Manchester Dry Docks. It had been bought by an investment company in 1971 who gave it the name Manchester Marine Ltd. The Ellesmere Port yard had previously closed in 1969 focussing operations at the original site above Mode Wheel. ML also acquired E Wilcox & Co (Chains) which specialised in lifting tackle. These companies working in collaboration with Morrell Mills and its Container Workshops Ltd provided valuable support both for ship and container maintenance.

Also by 1974, a full record of all containers was maintained by an in-house developed computer code with real time visual monitor display at all ML offices, both sides of the Atlantic and in the Mediterranean. This was an incredible technological achievement that was a decade ahead of the days of the personal computer.

The Manchester Liners' Board was very conscious that it had too many eggs in one basket and had resolved in the early 1970s to rectify this by building specifically for the charter market. There were insufficient medium-sized container ships and charter rates were attractive and steady, unlike the liner services which were undertaken at the very best at the behest of the dockers on both sides of the Atlantic. Two further ships of the **Manchester Challenge**-class were, therefore, ordered from Smith's Dock specifically for the charter market though also able to run on the Manchester to Montreal service with their quasi-sisters if required.

This pair was upgraded and modified from their forebears with operational experience from the four original ships. They were delivered by Smith's Dock in 1974. The *Journal of Commerce* headline cleverly ran '*Challenge with Courage brings Reward and Renown*'; the **Manchester Renown** being delivered in May and the **Manchester Reward** in October. Both ships were immediately chartered to the China Navigation Company (John Swire & Sons), for whom they served the next four years as the **Asian Renown** and **Asian Reward** respectively. The registered owner of the ships was Manchester Liners Intermodal Ltd, a protective measure should the charter market have failed. The deal was highly lucrative to Manchester Liners, bringing in a profitable reserve over and above the vessel's depreciation values. As a consequence a second pair of container ships was ordered from Smith's Dock, but these would be 17,000 tonners with over 800 TEU capacity. The success of the charter work was recognised by the second Queen's Award to the Company in 1976.

The **Manchester Reward** (1974) was built for the charter market and started life on charter as the **Asian Reward**.

[Fotoflite incorporating Skyfotos]

The first sailing from Manchester to Greece was undertaken by the chartered **Manchester Mercurio** on 18 January 1975. A sea and land container service to Iran, the Medliners-Iran service, was introduced via the Turkish port of Iskenderun and crossing only one border post on the four day journey on to Tehran. This was inaugurated by the chartered vessel **Manchester Falcon** in July. The same year ML flirted with a packaged and containerised housing manufacturer to form Manchester Adamson Ltd.

The steamer **Manchester Quest**, one time ugly duckling **Manchester Miller**, was sold for demolition in 1976. The **Manchester Concept**, former **Manchester Progress**, had earlier been sold to Mercantile Leasing Company of London and chartered back to ML. But 1976 also saw a significant new venture. In collaboration with the Alireza family of Jeddah, a jointly owned company named the Marine Transport International Company was created with ML holding just over one third of the assets. Under contract to Saudi Ports, the new company oversaw the development and subsequently managed the new container terminal at Berth 16 in Jeddah. The company went on to commission Berths 35 and 36 in subsequent years and was an excellent example of diversification based on detailed experience of port container handling by a shipping company. Work was also sought in India, but this was abandoned due to risk of non-payment, but subsequent work did take place in UAE at Sharjah.

Frank Narby's Cast operation, still a major shareholder in Manchester Liners, had not given up aspirations of owning ML outright. By June 1976 Cast had also acquired a 25% holding in Furness Withy and was demanding control of Manchester Liners via its surrogate part ownership of Furness Withy. Impasse reigned between Frank Narby's team and the Board of Furness Withy, with neither party talking to each other. In the meantime, the matter had been referred to the Monopolies and Mergers Commission. During the hearing held in summer 1976 the Eurocanadian Shipholdings plan was unveiled in which it wanted to combine its non-Conference service from Antwerp with calls at Liverpool to Montreal using the big 17,000 tonners ML had on order at Smith's Dock and intended to supplement the charter market. In October the Commission ruled against the merger stating: 'We consider that Manchester Liners is an effective company; in particular it has an impressive record of enterprise and innovation'. The report also highlighted the importance of Manchester Liners' integrated transport service which it offers to the shipper as opposed to the Cast port-to-port philosophy. Narby and his Cast brand resolved to put ships into Liverpool and then Avonmouth in an attempt to undermine Manchester Liners. At both ports the dockers, for once on ML's side, went on strike and the foreign ships were turned away.

The report of the Monopolies and Mergers Commission provides a succinct summary of ML's shipping activities as at 1976:

ML currently operates container ships which sail every five/seven days to Montreal from Manchester and once a month from Liverpool. Alternate Manchester sailings call at Greenock and the Liverpool sailing calls at Dublin. Despite the special design of the ships employed, the winter services are sometimes delayed by ice and bad weather, though ML claims less often than those of other operators using Montreal. The voyage from Manchester to Montreal, including the stop at Greenock, takes about seven and a half days in summer. The current total capacity of the service is of the order 30,000 TEU in each direction.

Besides the ordinary standard 20 foot containers ML also offers a variety of special containers suited to the requirements and conditions of the trade with Canada, such as half-height open-topped containers to carry metal bars. The filled containers can be delivered by the customer, either direct to the Manchester terminal or to ML's depots at Birmingham, Leicester, Belfast, Dublin and Glasgow. Alternatively ML offers its own transport service door to door. It also operates what is known as a 'less than one container load service' door to door in conjunction with National Carriers Ltd and Canadian National Railways; this service is known as Europex.

During the eight months 'open water season' ML operates a feeder service between Montreal and the Great Lakes ports such as Detroit, Cleveland, Milwaukee and Chicago. However, during the winter months, when the Great Lakes are frozen, freight has to be carried by rail and the two small container ships used on this service are then employed in the Mediterranean.

ML operates a small conventional North Atlantic service through an associate company, Golden Cross Line Ltd. This service caters for cargo which is not suitable for containerisation: it is the only British line serving Newfoundland.

ML operates four cellular container ships on two liner services to Mediterranean ports through a subsidiary company, Gough and Croswaite Ltd, whose sales and other functions are closely co-ordinated with the rest of the group. Sailings take place approximately every seven days serving Malta, Cyprus, Greece and Turkey, the Middle East and the Iberian Peninsular.

The road transport services referred to in the report were Wardell Warehousing and Wardell Transport Ltd, Warrington; Thomas Craig & Company, Glasgow; Waugh Road Services Ltd, Newcastle-upon-Tyne; and Commercial Cartage Ltd, east London.

The staffing of ML and its various associate companies in 1976 was quite considerable with 2,150 people employed directly, 170 of whom were located permanently overseas. Of the remainder, 440 staff were sea-going, 450 were in clerical support roles, 300 in land transport and 780 in engineering related roles.

The success of the charter to China Navigation Company had encouraged Manchester Liners to think even bigger. The **Manchester Renown** and **Manchester Reward** were the ultimate sized vessels to negotiate the Manchester Ship Canal, but the next pair, at over 17,385 tons gross, were far too large ever to see their port of registry. These were the **Manchester Vanguard** and **Manchester Venture**, and again built by Smith's Dock at a total cost of some £18 million. The **Manchester Vanguard** was registered under the ownership of the Golden Cross Line, and the **Manchester Venture** under Gough & Crosthwaite, the former shipbrokers that finally became ship owners. The arrival of the **Manchester Vanguard** into service was reported in *Sea Breezes*, November 1977:

With a length of 160 m and a beam of 23.2 m the **Manchester Vanguard** *can carry approximately 842 20 TEU, facilities being provided in certain holds and on deck for the carriage of 40 foot containers. Electrical sockets have been provided on deck for the carriage of thirty five 40 foot refrigerated containers. An interesting item is the installation of heeling tanks to port and starboard which are connected to an automatic pumping set and used to counteract heeling during loading and unloading of containers.*

A Scott-Sulzer 7-cylinder oil engine with a maximum output of 20,300 brake horse power at 122 revolutions per minute gives the ship a loaded speed of 20 knots. The machinery space is automated for unmanned operation.

The **Manchester Renown** (1974) was also built for the charter market.

[Fotoflite incorporating Skyfotos]

The **Manchester Vanguard** was the twelfth ship delivered to ML by Smith's Dock and there was light hearted talk of a 'bakers dozen'. Smith's entered into the spirit and presented ML with a 12 foot fibreglass sailing dinghy with her name, the **Manchester Charity**, emblazoned across her bows. The thirteenth ship was duly launched on Hollingworth Lake where Rob Stoker handed her over with due ceremony to the Sea Cadets. The fourteenth delivery to ML was the **Manchester Venture**, but she was paid for in full!

The **Manchester Vanguard** was immediately chartered to ACT (Associated Container Transportation - a consortium formed by Ben Line, Blue Star Line, Ellerman Line, Harrison Line and Port Line) and her maiden voyage was to Australia. Five months later in October the **Manchester Venture** was delivered and the pair was chartered for two years to Seatrain Lines, Inc, an American company registered in Monrovia, and adopted the names **Seatrain Trenton** and **Seatrain Bennington** respectively, along with full Seatrain livery. Just under two years later the pair reverted to their original names and, back in full ML livery, undertook a short season running between Liverpool and Montreal before adopting the names **Keelung** and **Marseille** on charter to the Gold Star Line of Hong Kong. With the charter completed, the pair moved to lay up in the Fal estuary in Cornwall in summer 1980. The bottom had by then completely fallen out of the charter market with a fast developing surplus of tonnage.

The **Manchester Vanguard** (1977) at the start of a charter to Associated Container Transportation (Australia), a consortium formed by the Ben Line, Blue Star, Cunard, Ellerman, Harrison and the Port Line.

[Author's collection]

With the return from charter of the **Manchester Reward** and **Manchester Renown** in 1978, the older **Manchester Challenge** and **Manchester Courage** were put on the For Sale list. The **Manchester Challenge** went first, adopting the name **Ocean Container** in 1978 and joined shortly afterwards by her sister which became **Pacific Container**. They were operated by the Hong Kong Island Shipping Company, although owned by separate organisations, and were registered in Panama. The **Frontier** was sold in 1979 to take up work in the Indian Ocean.

During 1978 ML said goodbye to Commodore Dennis Millard on his retirement and appointed Captain Alan Cookson as its new Commodore.

Company Chairman Tony Roberts, who had now succeeded Rob Stoker, reported a pre-tax loss of around £3.2 million for the year 1979:

During the first two months of the year [1979] the road haulage strike and secondary picketing resulted in the blockading of all UK Ports and brought the fleet to a standstill. This militant action by the labour unions took a toll upon the trade of our road haulage companies and the marine engineering group. Equally disappointing was the depressed world charter scene for those of our containerships made available on the market as the result of the lack of activity from the UK. These ships were chartered out together with our regular ships for the charter market, in a weak dollar earning currency...

Losses continued and eventually the nettle had to be grasped. Manchester Dry Docks Ltd, Morrell Mills & Company and Container Workshops Ltd, were placed in creditor's voluntary liquidation, E Wilcox & Co (Chains), was sold and James Walker & Sons (Shipping) was closed down.

Manchester Dry Docks' floating pontoon was broken up in 1979 while the three dry docks were put on a care and maintenance footing. A management buy-out eventually put two of the dry docks back into commission under the trading name United Ship Repairers and Engineers (Manchester) Ltd. The third dry dock was later leased by Stretford Shipbreakers and for a while the site remained in gainful employ.

With recession following the industrial unrest of the 1970s, the picture was indeed gloomy. And worse, the political upheaval suffered in Iran put the Medliners-Iran service out of kilter, with ML eventually withdrawing. On a brighter note the UK/Mediterranean Container Conference was started in 1979 in order to tackle over-tonnage on the various routes. Manchester Liners was a founder member of the Conference. The name Manchester Prince Line was retained through Gough & Crosthwaite but effectively ML operated the west coast services with Prince Line still trading out of London.

It was proposed to rationalise the five-ship service between Manchester and Montreal by moving from Manchester to Liverpool with a new service using new second generation ships that would allow a more economical three-ship service. The recession and events over which ML and Furness Withy had no control meant this vision was never to materialise. It also meant that ML would, in any event, abandon its container terminal at Manchester, putting a large nail into the coffin lid of deep water commercial activities at Manchester Docks.

The **Manchester Vanguard** berthed at the Brigham and Cowans shipyard in South Shields on 5 June 1982.

[Bernard McCall]

Mr Robert (Rob) Burdon Stoker (1914-2005)

Rob B Stoker, son of Kenneth Stoker, grandson of R B Stoker, was born at Hoylake and educated at Marlborough College. He joined Manchester Liners in 1932 working his way up through all the departments both at home and in Canada. During World War II, he was called up into the Royal Engineers and commissioned, then seconded to the Lower Clyde convoy assembly anchorage and later he went to North Africa, Sicily and the Adriatic as Deputy Ministry of War Transport Representative under Sir John Graham. Sir John later commended his flamboyant and often eccentrically over-dressed Deputy for his ability to get things done - tunnels were cleared and railways built.

In post-war years Rob Stoker took a leading role in developing the through services to the Great Lakes ports with the mini-Lakers and retained a keen interest in the developments leading up to the opening of the St Lawrence Seaway in 1959. He succeeded his father Kenneth Stoker as Managing Director in 1965 and as Chairman in 1968.

Kenneth had retained the Chair until then only so that his successor could devote time to his Presidency of the Manchester Chamber of Commerce and to help with the planning of the container services. Robert Stoker was champion of the containerisation programme and later creator of the Manchester Prince Line.

Robert Stoker retired from the Chair before the Furness Withy take-over by C Y Tung in 1979. Among his many other roles, he was a Director of Furness Withy, a Director of Charles Hill (Bristol City Line), President of the Manchester Steamship Owners Association, a regional Director of Barclays Bank and one time President of Cheadle Conservative Association. In addition he was actively involved with Salford University, the Mission to Seamen and the Manchester Port Welfare Board, Alderley Edge and Wilmslow Arthritis and Rheumatism Association, the St Ann's Hospice, the Boat Museum at Ellesmere Port and was an enthusiastic golfer. He received the MBE in 1998 for his work with St Ann's Hospice.

Robert Stoker's wife Mildred was the sponsor at the launch of the **Manchester Faith** in 1958. Mildred supported and encouraged her husband in his many endeavours and together they brought up three children. Succeeding Chairman and former Managing Director Tony Roberts spoke of his predecessor at his retirement with the following words:

Mr Stoker was a man of many parts, an author infused with a sense of history, appreciative of art and a painter himself, an orator with a gift for finding the right and imaginative phrase; a man with a genius for improvisation who followed his own judgement, intuition and impulse, a man of courage, of action and humanity, a leader who got things done; who produced and seized on new ideas and who was responsible for many nuggets of wisdom, talent, drive and genius.

Commenting on Mr Stoker's occasional outrageous headgear, Tony Roberts paused for a moment and added:

In fact these words were written about Sir Winston Leonard Spencer Churchill. If you thought I was referring to Mr Robert Burdon Stoker then, clearly, these two men share many characteristics.

CHAPTER 12

A 'CHINESE TAKE-AWAY' – THE TUNG TAKE-OVER

Headline news on the business pages of the *Manchester Evening News* on 14 February 1980 was 'Tung wants Furness'. The article began 'Last night Furness collected a surprise take-over bid from one of the most fascinating shipping men in the world, C Y Tung of Hong Kong'. On 17 March the Furness Withy Board unanimously agreed recommending acceptance of the 420p per share offer by Orient Overseas Containers (Holdings) Ltd., equivalent to a price of £112.5 million. OOCL by acquiring the majority issued shareholding in Furness Withy also collected the 61.6% Furness Withy holding in Manchester Liners. At the same time the 36.7% of Manchester Liners equity still held by Eurocandian Shipholdings (Cast) was bought at an agreed price of £10 million by C Y Tung subsidiary Rendish Investment Ltd making ML almost 100% Tung owned.

C Y Tung had successfully developed the Europe to Far East container trade with the Orient Overseas Container Line. He had also acquired a stake in the Dart Container Line operating between Europe and North America and Tung had services operating to Australia and the Middle East as well as a large tanker fleet. Assurances were given that the Furness group of companies would be left to develop as a major entity, staffed in the UK, with ships manned by British personnel under the Red Ensign. Tony Roberts optimistically responded on behalf of Manchester Liners with a statement that read:

The C Y Tung Group, together with Furness Withy, will be helping the company to continue developing its container service on the North Atlantic route as well as other activities – but, as usual, our future will rest on our own efforts.

How wrong he turned out to be. Meantime, Cast invested its £10 million unwisely and was all but bankrupt when it had to be reformed by the banks as Cast (1983) Ltd. The days of Cast's cut throat freight rates were very nearly over and in due course it applied to join the Conference. But in the short term competition from the Cast Line continued to hurt Manchester Liners with its non-Conference bargain basement freight rates. Depressed charter rates continued to damage income from the ships chartered out although charters in for the Mediterranean service were attractive. As a consequence the **Manchester Vigour** and **Manchester Zeal** were both sold in favour of chartered vessels in 1980 and 1981 respectively. In addition fighting in Lebanon was inhibiting trade with the eastern Mediterranean area while calls were finally reinstated in Italy.

The **Manchester Zeal** (1973) on charter to Cargo Lines.

[Fotoflite incorporating Skyfotos]

The chartered **Manchester Shipper** (1973) was one of several vessels used on the Mediterranean services in the mid-1970s.

[Author's collection]

1981 started badly with a seamen's strike bringing all the container services to a standstill. Margins on the transatlantic container services were nearly as low as the early years of 1971 and 1972 and the ML Board determined to take action. It resolved that rather than competing with CP Ships and Dart Container Line that were its main competitors, it would talk to them with the objective of some form of rationalisation of services. Canadian Pacific had three first-generation container ships in service on the North Atlantic, the **CP Discoverer**, **CP Trader** and **CP Voyageur**. With the greatly enhanced land catchment of the container, these ships were a real threat to ML's own trade.

The **CP Discoverer** (1971) was one of a trio of first generation cellular container ships operated by Canadian Pacific in direct competition with ML.

[Author's collection]

Although CP Ships pedigree was well known from its railway parentage and its famous main line Empress and subordinate Duchess liners, the ancestry of the Dart Container Line is less well known. In 1969 The Bristol City Line, a long standing friend of Manchester Liners operating to Canada from Bristol Channel ports, Compagnie Maritime Belge and Clarke Traffic Services formed a consortium under the Dart banner.

They commissioned four second generation 20 knot cellular container ships in the early 1970s: **Dart America**, **Dart Europe**, **Dart Atlantic** and **Dart Canada**. The Bristol City Line share was acquired by the Bibby Line in 1972 and then bought by CY Tung in 1980. CY Tung also acquired the Clarke interests to become the majority owner of Dart by 1980.

Unsurprisingly, given the majority Tung interest in both Manchester Liners and Dart, Manchester Liners, Dart Containerline (Canada) and CP Ships announced plans for a new co-ordinated weekly container service to Montreal out of Felixstowe and loading also at Hamburg, Antwerp and Le Havre. The service, to be named the St Lawrence Co-ordinated Service, would require four 1800 TEU ships (the entire Dart fleet) instead of the eleven operated by the three separate companies and was set to start in August 1981. The deal meant the withdrawal of Manchester Liners' container services to Montreal from the northwest of England and Greenock, while Southampton and Tilbury also lost services.

While the four ships were refitting and being ice strengthened, the **Manchester Vanguard** in company with the **Manchester Concorde** were honoured with opening the new route. The ships dedicated to the service were ready to take over within a few weeks. Manchester Liners chartered the former **Dart America** from her registered owners, the Tynedale Shipping Company, and renamed her **Manchester Challenge**; CP Ships the **CP Ambassador**, formerly the **Dart Atlantic**, and owned by Bristol City Line; and, the Dart Line through their partner Compagnie Maritime Belge (Lloyd Royal) S A contributed the Belgian-flagged **Dart Europe**. The fourth ship was the slightly smaller **Canadian Explorer**, formerly **Dart Canada**, which was put under joint management of ML, CP Ships and Dart Container Line.

Bristol City Line's **Dart Atlantic** (1971), complete with the Bristol company's blue star on white ground emblem on the bows, became the **CP Ambassador** under charter to Canadian Pacific for the St Lawrence Co-ordinated Service.
[Author's collection]

The first of the new ships to go on the service was the **Manchester Challenge** which arrived at Felixstowe from Hamburg and Antwerp during the first week of October resplendent in full ML livery and which sailed via Le Havre to Montreal under Captain John Mckay.

Tony Roberts explained:

With the current background conditions on the North Atlantic Manchester Liners had a very uncertain future because of the size of its vessels and the restricted market of the UK… The whole concept of this new venture is that the three companies will continue exactly as before by way of marketing and selling with a view to retaining and hopefully expanding their share of the market, each providing their usual back-up services such as documentation, container control and inland transportation.

Clearly the venture was not as co-ordinated as it could have been and meant ML again going back into Europe to sell its services – a task it had found profoundly difficult in 1973 (Chapter 11). But clearly also, closer integration between the partners, at least the Tung owned partners, could also mean ultimately cutting ML out of the deal – no easy waters for the ML Directors to attempt to steer through. Furness Withy at this time put its ship owning ventures under one office based in Manchester and made Tony Roberts Deputy Manager of the new Furness Withy Shipping Division. Manchester Liners House became Furness House and ML started along a slippery slope from which there would be no recovery.

The **Manchester Challenge** (1970), formerly the **Dart America**.

The **Manchester Concorde** (1969) was one of the original prototype cellular container ships but was good enough to start the St Lawrence Co-ordinated Service.

[both Fotoflite incorporating Skyfotos]

The remaining four Manchester Ship Canal sized container ships were sold rapidly thereafter. The **Manchester Concept**, formerly the **Manchester Port**, had left company service in 1980 having been chartered from a finance company since 1973. The **Manchester Concorde** and **Manchester Crusade** went to Chinese owners as the **Char Che** and **Char Lian** respectively, following approval from the Export Credits Guarantee Department of the Board of Trade. They were resold for demolition within the year. The **Manchester Renown**, which had only just been bought outright from Beaver Industries, was sold to Indonesian operators, and the **Manchester Reward**, which had some successful charters to Seatrain and others in 1979, stayed in the Tung empire eventually adopting the name **OOCL Award**, ultimately going for demolition in 1997.

The **Manchester Vanguard** and **Manchester Venture** were working for Mr Tung as the **Oriental Vanguard** and **Oriental Venture** and, following various name changes, were eventually sold to a company registered in Belize in 2000 for further service.

The **Manchester Vanguard** (1977) was too big ever to negotiate the Ship Canal to her home port.

[Fotoflite incorporating Skyfotos]

The same rationalisation process reformed the Mediterranean services. The Manchester Prince Line and Prince Line (London) were brought under one management and talks were held with the Conference competitors in the Mediterranean container trades. ML and Ellerman City Lines already collaborated in some areas, for example, Ellerman sending ML containers to Portugal, with the sole purpose of driving away the competition. Then in 1983 Manchester Liners/Prince Line approached Ellerman City Lines and Zim Israel Navigation Line with the idea of forming a non-competitive collaboration. The outcome was the Combined Container Service dedicated to two services, one centred on London, the other on Ellesmere Port, already the base for Ellerman and Zim, with calls at Dublin. With Manchester Liners' Mediterranean service moving down the canal to Ellesmere Port, the container terminal at No 9 Dock fell into disuse and for the first time in 85 years the ML house flag was no longer seen in Salford Docks.

The chartered **Manchester Trader** (1991) at Malta loaded with Ellerman Line and OOCL containers. Her charter ended in 1992 and with it also went the very last ship of the line.

[Author's collection]

By 1985 C Y Tung had bought out Compagnie Maritime Belge so increasing its stake in Dart and the joint service from Felixstowe. The Manchester Liners part of the Mediterranean service was maintained by the **Manchester Crown**, built as Prince Line's **Crown Prince** and the chartered German flag **Manchester Trader**, both of which were replaced by new chartered vessels, another **Manchester Trader** and the **Manchester City** later in the year. Manchester Liners found itself thoroughly boxed in by its own 'boxes' but more particularly by the Tung Group.

Following the global slump in trade in the early 1980s and with mounting debts, the Tung Group was forced to restructure in 1988. Manchester Liners' interests in the St Lawrence Co-ordinated Service were absorbed within the Orient Overseas Container Line banner and the **Manchester Challenge** was repainted in OOCL colours and given the name **OOCL Challenge**. At a stroke Manchester Liners had left the North Atlantic and the St Lawrence. Hardly a comment was made in the press, no fanfare was heard from the burghers of Montreal, no obituary appeared in the *Manchester Evening News*. Its downfall stemmed from two factors. The first was the continued dockside labour disputes on both sides of the Atlantic during the 1970s. The second was that the pioneering first generation container ships of the **Manchester Challenge** class were outpaced after only a couple of years by larger vessels introduced in the North Atlantic by other operators (such as the Dart Container Line) in the early 1970s.

The Manchester Prince Line interests also disappeared within the Tung dynasty in 1988 and Manchester Liners ceased to exist as a tangible and visible entity. Chartered vessels with Manchester names and capacity of little over 200 TEU, including one **Manchester Prince** and two more named **Manchester Trader**, continued out of Ellesmere Port and Dublin until they too returned to their owners in 1989 and 1992 respectively.

The Furness Withy component of the Tung Group was seen as the jewel in the crown and was protected from being broken up in a fire sale. Eventually, negotiations led to its purchase by Hamburg Sud Amerika for US$130 million in October 1990. Manchester Liners was no more, although it did briefly become a ship owner again in 1996 when the large gas tanker **Darwin** needed a temporary tax haven! The Furness Withy name survives within the Hamburg-Süd group and is principally engaged in offshore oil development and gas carriers.

But Manchester Liners did manage to outlive Manchester Docks, which effectively closed to commercial shipping in 1982. Currently owned by Peel Holdings, much of the Canal Company land has been sold and the Salford Dock Estate transformed into the Salford Quays featuring upmarket housing and leisure facilities. The Lowry art complex is at the end of the pier between Nos. 8 and 9 docks and the Imperial War Museum is located on the former Trafford Wharf. Furness House, formerly Manchester Liners House, still stands between the heads of Nos. 8 and 9 docks as a defiant reminder of the past. Trafford Park remains a major industrial complex and still hosts some of its long-standing investors. Kelloggs still manufactures its Corn Flakes on the same site it has operated since 1938 on Barton Dock Road, although much of the rest of the Park has been redeveloped and is better known nowadays as host to the Trafford Centre shopping complex.

When in 1979 Tony Roberts succeeded Robert Stoker as Chairman, his comments on the containerisation programme equally provide a sound epitaph for Manchester Liners Limited:

We did it. If we had failed it would have been the end. But if we had not done it we would have failed.

The old and the new: A coffee cup by Dunn Bennett & Company of Burslem, the gold ornamentation almost licked completed away, and the new, 'Steelite' from Royal Doulton.

[Author's collection]

Memories of ML

Many of us hold very different memories of Manchester Liners. The Manchester Liners Old Shipmates Association provides a valuable forum for former employees to keep in touch and exchange those memories. But for many others the memories stem just from seeing the Liners coming up and down the Manchester Ship Canal, the sight of the **Manchester Mariner** waist high in a Cheshire field of barley is one of the classic images.

I shudder to think just how many hours were spent standing on the footbridge over the Bridgewater Canal beneath the Power Station at Barton. Would the **Manchester Faith** come round the corner of the Ship Canal beyond Irlam Park Wharf, and the **Manchester Merchant** rise slowly up in Barton lock downstream of the Barton Bridges as promised in that morning's *Journal of Commerce*? There was the excitement of peering down the funnel of the **Manchester Shipper** as she hissed quietly beneath the Warburton High Level Bridge as the watcher disappeared in a haze of oil smoke. In later years there was the impressive sight of the red-hulled **Manchester Challenge** coming through Latchford lock with her bright red boxes. These are memories indeed.

The watcher also learned a little about hydraulics. The propeller of a big ship is designed to push water away from it in order to propel a ship forwards. In a confined channel the big Manchester Liners pushed the water away behind them, dragging water from the canal in front. The big ships had a momentum all of their own because they were always sailing downhill in the Canal into the reduced head of water in front from the increased head of water behind. It was always a thrill to watch this phenomenon from the bank looking up at the bulging sides of the pre-war **Manchester City** and her class-mates. It started with a wave from one of the crew on the forward tug and was followed by a wave from the Chief at the bow of the big ship. In *Sea Breezes*, May 1992, your author reported what happened next in an article entitled 'Manchester and its Liners':

At only a modest walking pace the ships set up quite a wave along the canal banks. The water rolled out ahead of the ship to expose a narrow black and oily foreshore. As the stem of the ship passed by the bow wave would slam into the bank, releasing a smell of used engine oil and other less desirable odours. The water was black, turbid, sometimes frothy and always vile... The filth left an oily tide mark along the red boot topping of the Manchester Liners – but it looked far worse on Harrison Line's pink.

The **Manchester Faith** outward bound and passing sedately through the Cheshire countryside on 13 October 1962. Such an image brings the memories flooding back.

[Bernard McCall]

REFERENCES

A number of newspapers and journals contain valuable historical insight into the activities of Manchester Liners. These include the *Journal of Commerce* and *Manchester Guardian*, latterly *The Guardian*, *Gazette* [Montreal] the monthly magazine *Sea Breezes*, the ML house magazine *Manchester Liners News* and the Furness Withy house magazine *The Log*.

Bruce W J 1990. *With the Manchester Ship Canal Company*. Neil Richardson, Radcliffe, Manchester.

Burrell D 1992. *Furness Withy, the centenary history of Furness Withy & Company 1891-1991*. World Ship Society, Kendal.

Burrell D 2000. "Manchester Liners Ltd" in *British Shipping Fleets (pp 6-71)* Editors: R Fenton & J Clarkson, Ships in Focus Publications, Longton.

Cudahy B J 2006. *Box boats: how container ships changed the world*. Fordham University Press.

Laird D 1961. *Paddy Henderson*. George Outram & Co., Glasgow and London.

Leech B 1907. *History of the Manchester Ship Canal – from its inception to its completion*. Sherratt & Hughes, Manchester and London.

Manchester Education Committee 1938. *The inland port of Manchester, its ships and their cargoes*. Port of Manchester Committee of the Manchester Chamber of Commerce, Manchester.

Pilgrim M 2010. *The memoires of Virginia Lord*. CreateSpace, Amazon.com.

Stoker R B 1959. *Sixty years on the Western Ocean*. Manchester Liners Ltd., Manchester.

The Monopolies and Mergers Commission 1976. *Eurocanadian Shipholdings Limited and Furness Withy & Company Limited and Manchester Liners Limited: a report on the existing and proposed mergers*. HMSO, London.

Wood C J 2005. *Manchester's Ship Canal, the big ditch*. Tempus Publishing, Stroud.

The ***Manchester Reward*** laid up in the River Fal on 29 July 1981, sixteen days after arrival. She later moved to the River Blackwater before sailing to Melbourne in late October.

[Bernard McCall]

MANCHESTER LINERS LIMITED

Name	Service years	Gross tons	History
Manchester Enterprise	1898-1899	3,878	Built 1890 as Queensmore for Steamship Queensmore Ltd; 1896 sold to Elder Dempster & Co; 1898 to ML; 1899 foundered on passage Liverpool to Montreal.
Manchester Trader	1898-1912	3,318	Built 1890 as Parkmore for Steamship Parkmore Ltd; 1897 sold to Elder Dempster & Co; 1898 to ML; 1912 sold to Akties Ferdinard Melson, Christiana and renamed Ferdinand Melson; 1914 sold to H Westfal Larsen, Bergen, and renamed Kaupanger; 1916 sunk by torpedo on passage Cardiff to Spezia.
Manchester City	1898-1929	7,696	Ordered by Furness Withy, delivered to ML; 1929 demolished.
Manchester Port	1899-1900	5,658	Sold to Robert Houston, London and renamed Hydaspes; 1930 demolished.
Manchester Corporation	1899-1929	5,467	Demolished.
Manchester Commerce	1899-1914	5,363	Sunk by mine on passage Manchester to Montreal.
Manchester Importer	1899-1927	4,028	Sold to Paul Negroponte, Syra, and renamed Alexandra; 1933 demolished.
Manchester Merchant	1900-1903	5,657	Caught fire and scuttled in Dingle Bay on passage New Orleans to Manchester.
Manchester Shipper	1900-1930	4,076	Demolished.
Manchester Exchange	1901-1925	4,091	Sold to A/B Finland Amerika Linjen O/Y, Helsinki and renamed Equator; 1939 sold to S A Cantiere di Porto Venere, La Spezia, renamed Caporto and demolished.
Manchester Market	1902-1903	4,091	Wrecked on passage Manchester to Philadelphia.
Manchester Engineer	1902-1916	4,302	Sunk by torpedo on passage Philadelphia to Manchester.
Manchester Inventor	1902-1917	4,247	Sunk by gunfire on passage St John to Manchester.
Manchester Spinner	1903-1918	4,227	Sunk by torpedo on passage Java to UK.
Manchester Miller	1903-1917	4,234	1905-1908 renamed Fulham; 1917 sunk by torpedo on passage Manchester to Philadelphia.
Manchester Merchant	1904-1920 1930-1933	4,152	1920-1930 ownership transferred to Manchester Ocean Services; 1933 demolished.

Name	Service years	Gross tons	History
Manchester Port	1904-1920	4,093	Transferred to Manchester Ocean Services; 1925 sold to H Vogemann, Hamburg, and renamed *Vogesen*; 1940 sunk by mine off Swedish coast.
Manchester Mariner	1904-1920	4,106	Transferred to Manchester Ocean Services; 1925 sold to A/B Finland Amerika Linjen O/Y, Helsinki, and renamed *Mercator*; 1939 sunk by torpedo on passage Rio de Janeiro to Finland.
Manchester Citizen	1912-1917	4,251	Sunk by torpedo on passage St John to Manchester.
Manchester Civilian	1913-1933	4,706	Sold to SG Razis, Argostoli, and renamed *Tasis*; 1935 sold to Myrtoon SS Co, Piraeus; 1940 seized by Vichy French and renamed *Equateur*; 1942 sold to Italian Government and renamed *Bari*; 1943 sinking and beached in Naples Roads.
Manchester Hero	1916-1937	5,738	Sold to Barry Shipping Co and renamed *St Winifred*; 1938 bombed and declared constructive total loss; 1938 sold to Compagnia Genovese di Navigazione a Vapore SA, Genoa, and renamed *Capo Vita*; 1941 sunk by torpedo on passage Naples to Tripoli.
Manchester Trader	1916-1917	3,985	Built 1902 as *Auchenblae* for Purdie, Glen & Co, Glasgow; 1916 to ML; 1917 sunk by gunfire on passage Suda Bay to Algiers.
Manchester Commerce	1916-1917	4,144	Built 1906 as *King* for State SS Co, Liverpool; 1916 to ML; 1917 sunk by torpedo on passage Cardiff to Gibraltar.
Manchester Engineer	1916-1917	4,415	Built 1906 as *Craigvar* for West of Scotland SS Co, Glasgow; 1913 sold to Treasury SS Co, Liverpool, and renamed *Nation* the following year; 1916 to ML; 1917 sunk by torpedo on voyage Newcastle to St Nazaire.
Manchester Inventor	1917 only	4,112	Built 1907 as *Celtic King* for Celtic Shipping Co, Liverpool; 1917 to ML; 1917 sunk by gunfire on passage Archangel to Belfast.
Manchester Brigade	1918-1940	6,021	Sunk by torpedo on passage Manchester to Montreal.
Manchester Division	1918-1953	6,027	Demolished.
Manchester Producer	1921-1939	6,576	Built 1916 as *Start Point* for Norfolk and North American SS Co, London; 1921 to ML; 1939 sold to Board of Trade, London and renamed *Botwey*; 1941 sunk by torpedo on passage Ellesmere Port to Port Sulphur.
Manchester Spinner	1921-1944	4,767	Built 1917 as *Grampian Range* for Neptune Steam Navigation Co, London; 1921 to ML; 1944 sold to Ministry of War Transport and scuttled off Juno Beach for Normandy Landings.
Manchester Regiment	1922-1939	7,930	Sunk in convoy collision.
Manchester Commerce	1925-1952	5,328	Sold to Camel Lines Ltd, London, and renamed *Corbita*; 1952 sold East and West SS Co, Karachi, and renamed *Fakirjee Cowasjee*; 1967 demolished.

Name	Service years	Gross tons	History
Manchester Citizen	1925-1943	5,328	Sunk by torpedo on passage Freetown to Lagos.
Manchester Exporter	1929-1947	5,277	Built 1918 as **Rexmore** for Johnston Line Ltd, London; 1928 transferred to Furness Withy & Co, London; 1929 to ML; 1947 sold to Cargueros Panamenos SA, Hong Kong and renamed **Nicaragua**; 1948 sold to Yu Chang SS Co, Shanghai, and renamed **Yu Tung**; 1950 sold to Wallem & Co, Hong Kong and renamed **Rio Bamba**; 1952 sold to TY Chao, Hong Kong, and renamed **Precila**; 1958 demolished.
Manchester Port	1935-1964	5,649 and post-war 7,170	Demolished.
Manchester City	1937-1964	5,600 and post-war 7,278	Demolished.
Manchester Progress	1938-1966	5,620 and post-war 7,375	Demolished.
Manchester Merchant	1940-1943	7,264	Sunk by torpedo on passage Manchester to Halifax.
Manchester Trader	1941-1963	5,671 and post-war 7,363	Demolished.
Manchester Shipper	1943-1969	7,881	Demolished.
Manchester Regiment	1947-1967	5,825 and later 7,375	Sold to Astro Tropica Compania Naviera SA, Panama, and renamed **Azure Coast II**; sold to Li-Ho Shipping, Singapore, no change of name; 1971 sold to United Maritime Management Co, Singapore, and renamed **Pu Gor**; 1971 demolished.
Manchester Merchant	1951-1967	7,651	Sold to Clio Shipping Co, Monrovia, and renamed **Clio**; 1972 on fire and sunk on passage Chittagong to Rotterdam.
Manchester Pioneer	1952-1963	1,805 post-1960 2,073	1960 lengthened; sold to United Maritime Enterprises SA, Panama, and renamed **Cyprian Med**; 1969 sold to Spanline Compania Naviera SA, Greece and renamed **Agios Antonius**; 1971 sold and renamed **Elentisas**, then demolished.
Manchester Explorer	1952-1963	1,805	Sold to Chimo Shipping Ltd, St John's, Newfoundland, and renamed **C A Crosbie**; 1965 renamed **P M Crosbie**; 1968 sold to Panagos Shipping Co, Nicosia, and renamed **Panagos L**; 1971 sold to Sylvia Shipping Co, Nicosia, and renamed **Ypermachos**; 1973 sold to Argolis Shipping Co, Nicosia, and renamed **Emilia**; 1980 renamed **Tassos** and demolished.
Manchester Spinner	1952-1968	7,815	Sold to Estiai Compania Naviera SA, Piraeus, and renamed **Estia**; 1971 sank after fire on passage Mexico to Brazil.

Name	Service years	Gross tons	History
Manchester Prospector	1953–1960	1,400	Built 1947 as **Vigor** for S Ugelstads Rederi A/S, Oslo; 1953 to ML; 1960 sold to Chr. M Sarlis & Co, Piraeus, and renamed **Georgios**; 1972 sold to Lassea Special Shipping SA, Piraeus, and renamed **Aghios Nektarios L**; 1985 sold to Nicolau Nikolaos, Greece, and demolished.
Manchester Mariner	1955–1968	7,580	Sold to Mira Compania Naviera SA, Panama, and renamed **Ira**; 1974 sold to National Steel Corporation, Manila, and renamed **Panday Ira**; 1977 demolished.
Manchester Vanguard	1956–1963	1,662	Sold to GSNC, London, and renamed **Sheldrake**; 1968 sold to Mediterranean Lines, Haifa, and renamed **Bat Golan**; 1974 sold to Woodchuck Shipping Corporation, Panama, and renamed **Woodchuck**; 1974 sold to South Wind Shipping Co, Singapore, and renamed **Selatan Maju**; 1981 sold to Hai Lee Shipping & Trading Co, Panama. and renamed **Wihari**; 1985 demolished.
Manchester Venture	1956–1961	1,662	Sold to GSNC, London, and renamed **Philomel**; 1968 sold to Mediterranean Lines, Haifa, and renamed **Bat Tiran**; 1972 caught fire and beached on passage Rijeka to Haifa.
Manchester Faith	1959–1970	4,459	1965–1966 renamed **Cairnesk**; sold to Marlineas Oceanicas SA, Panama, and renamed **Ilkon Tak**; 1978 transferred to Ilkon Shipping Co, Sarasota; 1978 sold to Yakinthai Shipping Co SA, Panama, and renamed **Chryseis**; 1983 demolished.
Manchester Fame	1959–1970	4,462	1965–1966 renamed **Cairnglen**; sold to Marcaminos Surenos Navegacion SA, Panama, and renamed **Ilkon Niki**; 1978 transferred to Ilkon Shipping Co SA, Sarasota; 1979 sold to Tranquil Marine Inc, Panama, and renamed **Efi**; sold to Seatime Shipping Inc, Piraeus, and renamed **Panagis K**; 1986 demolished.
Manchester Miller/ Manchester Quest	1959–1976	9,297/ 10,149	1970 converted and renamed **Manchester Quest**; 1976 demolished.
Manchester Commerce	1963–1971	8,724	Sold to Yick Fung Shipping & Enterprises Co, Hong Kong, and renamed **Ber Sea**; 1975 sold to Chinese Government and renamed **Yangchun**; 1980 shelled in Shatt-el-Arab [Iraq/Iran War], declared total constructive loss and demolished.
Manchester City	1964–1971	8,734	Sold to Korea Shipping Corporation, Seoul, and renamed **Korean Winner**, 1978 sold to Jin Yang Shipping Co, Seoul, and renamed **One West No 8**; 1985 demolished.
Manchester Renown	1971 only	8,742	Built as **Manchester Renown** 1964 for Beaver Industries Ltd, London; 1971 to ML; sold to Korean Shipping Corporation, Seoul, and renamed **Korean Challenger**; 1978 sold to Witney Shipping Corporation, Panama, and renamed **Edessa**; 1984 demolished following engine room fire.
Manchester Exporter	1965–1969	7,506	Built 1952 as **Cairndhu** for Cairn Line of Steamships, Newcastle; 1965 to ML; sold to Halieto Oceania Naviera SA, Panama, and renamed **Gemini Exporter**; 1971 demolished.
Manchester Port	1966–1971	8,938	Sold to Jadranska Slobodna Plovidba, Split, and renamed **Biokovo**; 1980 sold to Vroulidia Compania Naviera SA, Panama, and renamed **Ydra**; 1983 demolished following engine room fire.

Name	Service years	Gross tons	History
Manchester Progress/ Manchester Concept	1967-1973	8,176/ 11,228	1971 converted and renamed Manchester Concept; 1973 sold to Mercantile Leasing Co, London; 1980 sold to Peninsula Shipping Co, Singapore, and renamed Cherry Bunga; 1985 demolished.
Manchester Challenge	1968-1978	12,039	Sold to Hong Kong Ccean Shipping Co and renamed Ocean Container; 1984 transferred to Hong Kong Champion Shipping Co SA, Hong Kong; 1989 renamed Hang Fu; 1989 sold to Glavish International Corporation, Panama, and renamed SC Susanna; 1992 renamed Swan 1; 1993 demolished.
Manchester Courage	1969-1979	12,039	Sold to Carolina Leasing Ltd, London, and renamed Pacific Container; 1984 transferred to Hong Kong Excellent Shipping Co, Panama; 1989 sold to Ginza Internationl Corporation, Panama, and renamed MSC Marina; 1992 renamed City of Limassol; 1992 demolished.
Manchester Merito/ Manchester Merit/ Fortuna	1970-1975	3,414	1970 completed as Catalina del Mar, renamed Manchester Merito then Manchester Merit in British register; 1972 renamed Fortuna; 1975 sold to Chelwood Shipping Ltd, Monrovia, and renamed Kathleen; 1987 renamed Kudu; 1990 sold to Societa Italiana di Navigazione, Naples, and renamed Cement Two; 1996 sold to Jukingor Marine Corporation, Panama, and renamed Fortune R; 1999 transferred to Cement Trading Inc, Panama, and renamed Libera; still in service 2010.

Manchester Concorde (1969) and Manchester Crusade (1971) were owned by the Nile Steamship Co, London, and demise chartered to ML, going to Furness Withy [Shipping] in 1982.

Numerous other vessels were chartered in, particularly from 1968 onwards. Some adopted Manchester names and full ML livery, others just ML funnel colours while some retained the markings of their owners.

STEAMSHIP KNUTSFORD LIMITED

Name	Service years	Gross tons	History
Knutsford	1903-1915	3,842	Ex R B Stoker 1903; 1913 sold to Gripwell SS Co, renamed Gripwell; 1914 repossessed and renamed Knutsford; 1914 sold to Leeds Fire Clay Co; 1916 sold to Woolston SS Co; 1916 sunk by gunfire on passage Tunis to Baltimore.

BRITISH AND ARGENTINE STEAM NAVIGATION COMPANY (FURNESS WITHY & CO after 1934) jointly with MANCHESTER LINERS LIMITED (Managers: Houlder Brothers & Company)

Name	Service years	Gross tons	History
El Argentino	1928-1937	9,501	1937 wholly owned by Furness Withy & Co, London; 1943 sunk by bombing on passage Glasgow to Montevideo.

MANCHESTER OCEAN SERVICES LIMITED

Name	Service years	Gross tons	History
Manchester Merchant	1920-1930	4,152	Built 1904 for ML; 1920 to MOS; 1930 returned to Manchester Liners; 1933 demolished.
Manchester Port	1920-1925	4,093	Built 1904 for ML; 1920 to MOS; 1925 sold to H Vogemann, Hamburg, and renamed **Vogesen**; 1940 sunk by mine off Swedish coast.
Manchester Mariner	1920-1925	4,106	Built 1904 for ML; 1920 to MOS; 1925 sold to A/B Finland Amerika Linjen O/Y, Helsinki, and renamed **Mercator**; 1939 sunk by torpedo on passage Rio de Janeiro to Finland.

CONDRONS (MANCHESTER) LIMITED

Name	Service years	Gross tons	History
Frontier	1972-1975	3,621	Transferred to Manchester Liners [Freighting] Ltd; 1979 sold to Bayworth Shipping Corporation, Monrovia and renamed **Box Trader**; 1984 sold to Wexford Shipping Co, Limassol and renamed **Haris**; 1985 demolished following engine room fire.

MANCHESTER LINERS (FREIGHTING) LIMITED

Name	Service years	Gross tons	History
Frontier	1975-1979	3,621	Built 1972 as **Frontier** for Condrons [Manchester] Ltd; 1979 sold to Bayworth Shipping Corporation, Monrovia, and renamed **Box Trader**; 1984 sold to Wexford Shipping Co, Limassol, and renamed **Haris**; 1985 demolished following engine room fire.

MANCHESTER LINERS (TRANSPORT) LIMITED

Name	Service years	Gross tons	History
Manchester Vigour	1973-1980	5,310	1976 renamed **Cargo Vigour** and later **Manchester Vigour**, sold to Compagnie Maritime d'Affretement, Marseilles, and renamed **Ville d'Orient**; 1984 sold to Islamic Development Bank, Abu Dhabi, and renamed **Benwalid**; 1997 sold to Pollux Shipping Lines Inc, Mumbai, and renamed **Pollux**; 1998 transferred to Luhum International Ltd, Road Town, British Virgin Islands; 1999 sold to Winnerwald Inc, Panama; still in service 2010.
Manchester Zeal	1973-1981	5,310	1975 renamed **Cargo Zeal**; 1976 renamed **Manchester Zeal**; 1981 to Pacific International Lines, Singapore, and renamed **Sea Hawk**; 1990 sold to Tanto Intim Lines PT, Surabaya, and renamed **Sea Leopard**; 1991 renamed **Kurnia Samudera**; 1993 sold to Pacific Lady Inc, Surabaya, and renamed **Pacific Lady**; 1996 renamed **Hub Usaha**; still in service 2010.

MANCHESTER LINERS (INTERMODAL) LIMITED

Name	Service years	Gross tons	History
Manchester Renown	1974-1982	12,577	1974 renamed *Asian Renown*; 1978 renamed *Manchester Renown*; 1982 sold to PT Perusahaan Pelayaran. Samudera Karana Line, Djakarta, and renamed *Ratih*; 1990 renamed *OOCL Amity*; 1993 renamed *Ratih*; 1995 demolished.
Manchester Reward	1974-1982	12,577	1974 renamed *Asian Reward*; 1978 renamed *Manchester Reward*; 1979 renamed *Seatrain Norfolk*; 1979 renamed *Manchester Reward*; 1980 renamed *Manchester Reward*; 1982 transferred by CY Tung to Famous Shipping SA, renamed *TFL Reward*; 1990 renamed *Manchester Reward*; 1991 transferred to Greenford Shipping Ltd, Monrovia, and renamed *OOCL Award*; and renamed *R R Ratna*; 1991 transferred to Greenford Shipping Ltd, Monrovia, and renamed *Award*; 1997 renamed *Award 1* and demolished.

The *Manchester Challenge* (1970) was owned by Tynedale Shipping Co, for Dart Containerline.

GOLDEN CROSS LINE LIMITED

Name	Service years	Gross tons	History
Manchester Vanguard	1977-1983	17,385	1977 renamed *Seatrain Trenton*; 1978 renamed *Manchester Vanguard*; 1979 renamed *Oriental Vanguard* for CY Tung; 1982 renamed *Ibn Majid*; 1983 transferred to Express Tanker Services, Bermuda, and renamed *Oriental Expert*; 1983 transferred to Chinese Maritime Transport Ltd, Taipei; 1991 transferred to Wellway Shipping, Hong Kong, and renamed *OOCL Applause*; 1994 renamed *Eagle Respect*; 1998 renamed *OOCL Applause*; 1998 transferred to Da Ling Shipping, Belize, and renamed *Da Ling*; 2002 demolished.

GOUGH & CROSTHWAITE LIMITED

Name	Service years	Gross tons	History
Manchester Venture	1977-1980	17,385	1977 renamed *Seatrain Bennington*; 1979 renamed *Manchester Venture*; 1979 renamed *Marseille*; 1980 renamed *Manchester Venture*; renamed *Oriental Venture* for CY Tung [Kalten Shipping, Hong Kong); 1981 renamed *Rhein Express*; 1984 renamed *Oriental Ambassador*; 1989 renamed *OOCL Alliance*; 1992 transferred to Chinese Maritime Transport Ltd, Hong Kong; 1996 transferred to Pacific Union Container Carriers Ltd, Hong Kong; 1999 renamed *Star Alliance* and then *OOCL Alliance*; 2000 sold to Da Sheng Shipping Ltd, Belize, and renamed *Da Sheng*; 2002 demolished.

INDEX OF MERCHANT SHIPS' NAMES

Manchester Shipper (1943) 34,41,64,65,69-72,76,81,
82,87,93,96,98,99,103,130,134
Manchester Shipper (1973) 115,125
Manchester Spinner (1903) 19,32,47,132
Manchester Spinner (1917) 36,39,58,62,133
Manchester Spinner (1952) 34,77-79,81,82,88,100,
102,134
Manchester Trader (1890) 8,9,14,25,132
Manchester Trader (1902) 31,34,133
Manchester Trader (1941) 61,62,72,76,78,94,95,134
Manchester Trader (1955) 95
Manchester Trader (1977) 128
Manchester Trader (1978) 128
Manchester Trader (1980) 129
Manchester Trader (1991) 128,129
Manchester Vanguard (1956) 46,83,85,89,92,135
Manchester Vanguard (1977) 120-122,126-128,138
Manchester Venture (1956) 46,83,92,135
Manchester Venture (1977) 120,121,127,138
Manchester Vigour (1973) 46,115,116,124,137
Manchester Zeal (1973) 46,115,124,137
Mandalay (1872) 17
Marseille (1977) 121,138
Mary P Cooper (1896) 92
May (1890) 17
Menominee (1897) 41
Mercator (1904) 133,137
Mongolian Prince (1913) 39,41
Mont Alta (1944) 82
MSC Mallard [tug] (1939) 54
MSC Marina (1969) 136
Nation (1906) 133
New York City (1956) 85
Nicaragua (1918) 71,134
Norman Prince (1956) 101
North Brook (1919) 85,86
Northwestern Miller (1915) 39
Ocean Container (1968) 121,136
Ocean Prince (1907) 26
Old Trafford [tug] (1907) 52
One West No 8 (1964) 135
OOCL Alliance (1977) 138
OOCL Amity (1974) 138
OOCL Applause (1977) 138
OOCL Award (1974) 127,138
OOCL Challenge (1970) 129
Oriental Ambassador (1977) 138
Oriental Expert (1977) 138
Oriental Vanguard (1977) 127,138
Oriental Venture (1977) 127,138
Oropesa (1920) 59
Oswestry Grange (1902) 21
P M Crosbie (1952) 92,134
Pacific Commerce (1922) 39
Pacific Container (1969) 121,136
Pacific Lady (1973) 137
Pacific Stronghold (1945) 69
Pacific Exporter (1928) 40
Panagis K (1959) 135
Panagos L (1952) 134
Panday Ira (1955) 135
Parkmore (1890) 8,9,132
Philomel (1956) 92,135
Planet Mars (1900) 21
Planet Mercury (1894) 21
Planet Neptune (1901) 20,21

Planet Venus (1900) 21
Politician (1923) 37
Pollux (1973) 137
Precila (1918) 134
Pu Gor (1947) 134
Queensmore (1890) 8,9,132
R B Stoker (1903) 136
R R Ratna (1974) 138
Ratih (1974) 138
Reindeer 1 (1883) 42
Rexmore (1918) 44,58,76,134
Rhine Express (1977) 138
Rhine Ore (1960) 117
Rio Bamba (1918) 134
Riverdale Park (1943) 65,69
S C Sussana (1968) 136
Saxilby (1914) 48
Sea Hawk (1973) 137
Sea Leopard (1973) 137
Seaboard Star (1944) 82
Seatrain Bennington (1977) 121,138
Seatrain Norfolk (1974) 138
Seatrain Trenton (1977) 121,138
Selatan Maju (1956) 135
Sheldrake (1956) 92,135
Sir John Crosbie (1962) 115
Southern Prince (1956) 92,93,95,98
Southwestern Miller (1915) 39
Spartan Prince (1954) 100
St Ola (1892) 11
St Winifred (1916) 51,133
Star Alliance (1977) 138
Start Point (1916) 36,37,133
Stockport (1911) 63
Straits of Menai (1894) 8,17
Straits of Sunda (1895) 17
Suffolk (1902) 18
Swan I (1968) 136
Sydenham (1891) 17,27
Tactician (1961) 114
Tartar Prince (1959) 100
Tasis (1913) 133
Tassos (1952) 134
TFL Reward (1974) 138
Titanic (1912) 20
Toronto City (1945) 85
Trojan Prince (1954) 100,101
Tusculum Victory (1945) 69
Vespasian (1887) 36
Vigør (1947) 79
Ville d'Orient (1973) 137
Vogesen (1904) 133,137
Volumnia (1911) 44,58
War Beryl (1918) 36
Western Prince (1955) 92,95
Westmount Park (1943) 65,69
Wihari (1956) 135
Woodchuck (1956) 135
Yangchun (1963) 135
Ydra (1966) 135
Ypermachos (1952) 134
Yu Tung (1918) 134
Zealandic (1955) 95

MANCHESTER MISCELLANY

The **Manchester Regiment** (1947) is seen in Canadian waters. Sadly we have neither date nor location for this photograph.

[World Ship Photo Library]

Another undated photograph in the Canadian ice. The subject is the **Manchester Mariner** (1955).

[World Ship Photo Library]

In stark contrast to the older vessels, the **Manchester Faith** was one of several German-built container ships to be chartered by Manchester Liners or Manchester Prince Line. She is an example of the Type 83 design from the J J Sietas shipyard near Hamburg and was delivered as **Francop** in 1974. She was chartered by ML in 1976/77 and again between 1978 and 1983. She is seen approaching Eastham on 28 August 1979.

[Laurie Schofield]

After being sold in autumn 1981, the **Manchester Concorde** (1969) arrived in Hull from Felixstowe on 29 October 1981 and was photographed soon after arrival on that date.

[Bernard McCall]

The Liverpool skyline has changed much since the **Manchester Challenge** (1970) was photographed heading towards the Manchester Ship Canal on 10 May 1977. The Anglican cathedral, however, remains a prominent landmark.

[Laurie Schofield]

Finally, we see the **Manchester Concept** (1967) in classic view as she approaches Eastham in readiness to enter the Manchester Ship Canal on 10 May 1978.

[Laurie Schofield]